BURLING1

MW01178614

service
LEADERSHIP

service LEADERSHIP

How Having a Calling Makes the
Workplace More Effective

RICHARD J. GOOSSEN
THEODORE ROOSEVELT
MALLOCH

Skyhorse Publishing

Skyhorse Publishing books may be purchased in bulk at special discounts for sales promotion, corporate gifts, fund-raising, or educational purposes. Special editions can also be created to specifications. For details, contact the Special Sales Department, Skyhorse Publishing, 307 West 36th Street, 11th Floor, New York, NY 10018 or info@skyhorsepublishing.com.

Skyhorse® and Skyhorse Publishing® are registered trademarks of Skyhorse Publishing, Inc.®, a Delaware corporation.

Visit our website at www.skyhorsepublishing.com.

10 9 8 7 6 5 4 3 2 1

Library of Congress Cataloging-in-Publication Data is available on file.

Cover design by Rain Saukas

Print ISBN: 978-1-5107-3527-9
Ebook ISBN: 978-1-5107-3528-6

Printed in the United States of America

TABLE OF CONTENTS

INTRODUCTION

This book is about work, spirituality, and leadership.

Most people already have a strong sense of what these words mean, but they struggle with how precisely to find the right balance between them in their lives. Employees on the job have a sense that all three are important, but they don't always find that they are able to actualize their pursuit of them in the course of a career—at least not equally. Employers, on the other hand, have the sense that all three are connected, but they struggle to find the right mix. Most assuredly, employers feel that open pursuit of spirituality in the workplace can take a business organization into dangerous territory.

This book has been written to address the *disconnect* between a corporation's attempt to establish—typically unilaterally—its own sense of meaning and purpose and an employee's need to find an overarching calling in their work . . . without feeling one has already been imposed by "Big Brother." Research shows an organization will not get the most out of its workforce unless it respects and facilitates each individual's framework for a pursuit of meaning. Often, this is done in the context of spirituality. "Service Leadership" is the title of this book, and it's a reference to serving employees' quests for purpose under the corporate umbrella.

Organizations that do not address existing core belief systems of employees will be disadvantaged in the marketplace. Organizations that do, on the other hand, stand to be richly rewarded for it with increased efficiency, productivity, and employee satisfaction. We recognize that significant energy is required to begin changing an organization—but, as this book will show, the resulting advantages will justify the effort.

WHO IS IT FOR?

This book is for business leaders (or future business leaders) at any level who run organizations and want to do so more effectively. This book outlines a *new* way to think about leading as service; and it will be a useful tool to anyone or any company that seeks to go down this path. This book is also for business people who have the sense that an element of spirituality and calling has been lost in the contemporary workplace and who also have the feeling that tremendous business advantages could be realized if this element were to be reintroduced in a workplace-appropriate way.

FAMILIARITY, BUT NOT UNDERSTANDING

Religious terminology has often been absorbed into general usage and contemporary corporate-speak, without any concomitant understanding. We use the words, but we don't know where they came from or what thy used to mean. To begin with an extreme example, there is the notion of "cult brands" and "cult following." Cults are typically understood as deviations from the norm, often with charismatic leaders who inspire extreme devotion among their followers. A leader may, in turn, be described as having a "messianic complex." Mark Zuckerberg, the cofounder and CEO of Facebook, has been described by a former employee as "Keeper of a messianic vision that, though mercurial and stinting on specifics, presents an overwhelming and all-consuming picture of a new and different world . . . . By imprinting this vision on his disciples, Zuckerberg founded the church of a new religion" (Bokhari, 2016). There are often business lists of top "cult brands" such as Google and Lululemon, both of which are discussed later in this book. In terms of company leaders, one common term in high-tech circles is "evangelist." This describes a person who is an advocate for the brand or the product and is particularly zealous. Some companies use such a formalized title while others refer to marketers using this mantle.

In corporate circles, there is often talk about the "soul" of the business or firm—in other words, what the company is about deep down. Experienced business consultants and authors John Izzo and Eric Klein (1997, p. 7) have described the "corporate soul" as "the experience of coming fully alive at work . . . foremost, an experience of touching a deeper level of vitality, inspiration, meaning, and creativity." They define soul as a term that "signifies the basic vital energy that underlies and animates all human activity" (p. 7). There is also the notion of guarding the soul. In a corporate context, the notion of "selling your soul" sometimes comes up. This is the well-known notion of a "Faustian bargain," which is an agreement with Evil, in the form of the Devil, often (as in the classical story of Faust) with the paradoxical intention of achieving a higher Good that is otherwise corrupted. What has the person making the agreement traded to the Devil? Can the person avoid being trapped? A pact with the Devil is dangerous, for the only thing the Devil is said to want is, in fact, the person's soul. Business leaders are warned!

Last but not least, the notion of "calling" is a once-religious concept that has definitely gone mainstream. Calling is all the rage because employees are looking for inner direction and satisfaction in their work lives, and they can relate to a focus or force that might compel them in their work. Business leaders are comfortable with calling because while it invokes a powerful motivation, this motivation is no longer *necessarily* religious.

Despite this superficial familiarity with religious concepts, any discussion of concepts that relate to religion and spirituality in a corporate context can be easily misunderstood and misinterpreted. And while there may be references to religious terminology, there remains a lack of accord when it comes to how best to treat religion or spirituality.

Religion often makes contemporary corporations nervous. Rather than viewing religion as something providing people with a sense of meaning, guidelines for good ethical behavior, a desire to serve, and a positive force in society, corporations can see it as dangerous, regressive, proselytizing, intolerant, and dogmatic—even something to be kept out of a corporate context. Company leaders will need to have a balanced view of religion and particular faiths—and people who hold none—in order to practice service leadership effectively. If your impressions of religion fall into the latter categories, don't worry! You're in the majority. This book will be a guide to taking the best parts of spirituality and calling and using them in the workplace, while still respecting your employees' spiritual privacy.

THE FOUNDATION OF THE RESEARCH IN THIS BOOK

To provide a quick overview at the outset, here is a quick guide to the methodology and practice that went into this project:

- The findings in this book are based—in large part—on exhaustive firsthand interview research. Senior company leaders have been interviewed over the past decade to provide the content in this book. Many of these interviews were secured through personal relationships and would not be readily available to most researchers.
- This research includes companies from all over the world and thus has a cross-cultural perspective. In the context of our discussion, like many others, what is reasonable in one context may not be within another. In the course of a discussion of service leadership, this book draws on insights from companies in Europe, North America, Africa, the Middle East, Asia, and Australia.

- Our knowledge of companies practicing service leadership is enhanced by firsthand experience working with companies throughout the world. The authors are actively engaged and working with companies' senior leaders in terms of strategic and board leadership.
- This book discloses company names when appropriate. In other cases, this book provides only summaries that describe the business and then its relevance to our discussion of service leadership.
- In some cases, this book simply offers a "composite sketch" of a company to illustrate how a company could reflect various aspects of service leadership. There may be a composite of companies to represent a field, (e.g., a professional services firm).
- A number of companies have relevant insights related to difference aspects of our overall model and will be referred to more than once.

AUTHOR CAVEATS: RELIGION AND WORKPLACE SPIRITUALITY

Before we embark on our detailed analysis in the following chapters, We'd like to state two caveats. This is done to ensure that there is clarity around our argument—and to point out what we are *not* talking about.

First, to be clear, this book is not promoting any particular religion or ideology. It is, however, arguing that there should be an appreciation of the role of religion or spirituality in the lives of employees. These things are a fundamental part of the general human condition.

A second caveat concerns "workplace spirituality." Workplace spirituality involves advocating for the role of spirituality in the workplace, the importance of individuals' spiritual dimension and the role of a supportive community. This could include various multifaith initiatives such as providing a prayer room or employing a multifaith chaplain. However, this book is not connected to this notion of "workplace spirituality." It is not advocating for more or less spirituality in the workplace. Instead, it is advocating for an environment that respects and understands frameworks for meaning, recognizes that they are deeply held, recognizes that this is the context in which individuals approach meaning at work, and recognizes that they should not be impinged upon. This liberal and market-based approach is actually positive for people with a clear framework of meaning, wherever it is derived from, religious or not.

Now, with these caveats out of the way, let's begin by looking at service, sensemaking, and calling in the workplace.

CHAPTER 1

SERVICE, SENSEMAKING, AND CALLING

Meaning in life and meaning at work

The importance of meaning at work

Sensemaking, calling, and meaning within organizations

The outline of the argument

MEANING IN LIFE AND MEANING AT WORK

Most discussions of finding meaningfulness in work are held in a vacuum. That is to say, meaning is discussed as though it can only happen between 8 a.m. and 5 p.m. But there are many things outside of work that give our lives meaning. Omitting these elements from discussions of what makes work meaningful is a big problem.

Work is a critically important part of life—and, true, for some it may indeed be the most significant part of a life—but it still must be discussed in conjunction with meaning that can be found in other times and places.

People generally enter the full-time workforce between their late teens and late 20s, depending upon their amount of training and formal education. And people generally exit full-time employment between their late 50s and their early 70s. There's also an average of 20 years of living at either end when people aren't working. But in that middle, people spend 40–60 hours at work each week. That comes to about 35 percent of their total time, at least in the Western world. That's a lot, but it isn't everything.

People develop mental frameworks for making sense of the world and their place in it, including the place of the work that they do. This is seemingly the core nature of people or personhood. Jose Ortega y Gasset, a Spanish philosopher, once noted in his book *Man and Crisis*, "How can anyone live if we silence these ultimate dramatic questions? Where does the world come from, and where is it going? What is the supreme power of the cosmos? What is the essential meaning of life?"

There are many ways of attempting to answer these questions articulated by Ortega y Gasset. In most countries and societies, religion and a religious framework has played a crucial role in finding those answers. Alistair McGrath, Professor of Science and Religion at the University of Oxford, in his book *Mere Apologetics*, suggests that

Religion comes naturally to us—sometimes in the form of a fascination with the "transcendent", sometimes through a sense of presence or agency, sometimes through a sense of something ultimate beyond the realm of reason and experience, and sometimes through an awareness of our place within a deeper order of things. That is why we cannot stop talking about ultimate questions—such as God and the meaning of life. We seem to be meant to ask such questions (McGrath, 2015, p. 184).

So when we talk about work having meaning—indeed, when we are talking about meaning at all—we're talking about a sphere that necessarily has to do with religion. We have to accept this. Many contemporary workplaces find it distasteful or troubling to talk about work and religion together. However, every employee is ultimately a meaning-seeking individual who is wrestling with what the role of work is in his or her lives.

Viktor E. Frankl, author of the massively influential *Man's Search for Meaning* (1959), has skillfully summarized the importance of this search. Frankl survived the horrors of Nazi concentration camps of World War II. In doing so, he learned that the survivors were not the most physically strong camp inmates, but rather those who had found some purpose to live for beyond their present circumstances. When the war ended, Frankl developed this idea into the concept of "logos therapy." Believing that people who had a "why" could endure any "how," Frankl concluded that

Man's search for meaning is the primary motivation in his life and not a "secondary rationalization" of instinctual drives. This meaning is unique and specific in that it must and can be fulfilled by him alone; only then does it achieve a significance which will satisfy his own *will* to meaning (Frankl, 1959, p. 121).

Frankl also made the case that meaning—including deep, existential meaning—could be pursued and considered apart from what we would today call established religion. In other words, Frankl would say that we are able to embrace the value of the pursuit of meaning without needing to employ or identify with a particular religious framework.

Another perspective on meaning is provided by Stephen Green, in the UK. Lord Green is former chairman and CEO of the Hong Kong and Shanghai Banking Corporation (HSBC), a global financial services institution with $80 billion USD in annual revenue. During his time at the helm, HSBC had 300,000 employees and generated $20 billion in annual profits. Lord Green is also an ordained minister in the Church of England, and the author of books on subjects ranging from German history to modern-day financial markets. In a chapter titled "In My End is My Beginning," in one of his books entitled *Good Value* (2009), he states, "The goal [in life] is a completeness we will never achieve; but the journey is all-important. The end is clear, and it defines how we must begin." As Green further notes in the same work, "Neither money nor ambition nor serendipity is good enough as a work/life principle. We have to find a better answer to the question: Why do I do what I do? . . . The answer matters. We have only one life." Here again we see the connection. Work, life, and a deep quest for meaning—all are linked. All are inextricable.

Any organization is composed of people—employees, volunteers, and so forth. And virtually all of these people are seeking meaning in their lives. Since work is where people spend many of their waking hours and much of their intellectual energy—and is often where and how they derive their identities—a truly effective organization must understand how to address this omnipresent need for meaning. The most successful companies are the ones that actively engage with how their approach works on an existential level.

There are many in the business world who operate on the idea that money is the only (or at least primary) motivator of an employee. This is not an altogether safe assumption. People are not simply economic maximizers. Identity matters. Culture matters. How they spend their time matters. People want more out of life than only a paycheck, and this is, time and again, reflected in their decision making. Further, these motivations vary with each generational cohort, as we discuss throughout the book. Put plainly, people make decisions that do not make economic sense, and they do this all the time.

Why not automatically move if a job in another city will pay a higher salary? Why not do something that you know you don't like—in order to make more money? Why not travel incessantly and never see your family—in order to make more money?

We all know the answers to these questions already. There is more to life. There is meaning.

Workers are increasingly connecting their decision making with their meaning-making priorities.

So, if this is the case, we are forced to arrive at the following question: how is the pursuit of meaning achieved in a relationship between employees and the companies they work for?

THE IMPORTANCE OF MEANING AT WORK

Meaning at work cannot be separated from the consideration of meaning in life. The two are connected, and employers should embrace this fact with open arms. For, if the two are in sync, employees will be far more motivated.

Most people accept the following as common sense: "The more meaning, purpose, and significance you can ascribe to your work, the more likely it is you'll work harder, be more productive and successful, and enjoy it along the way" (Yoon, 2014). But if this is so obvious, why isn't it being practiced by more organizations? It's a question we need to answer. There are some fundamental gaps in how organizations work with employees, which have costly consequences for engagement, productivity, and enthusiasm.

Over the past few years, a few authors *have* tried to engage with this search for meaning under different names. As Amabile and Kramer (2012) note in a *McKinsey Quarterly* article,

As a senior executive, you may think you know what Job Number 1 is: developing a killer strategy. In fact, this is only Job 1a. You have a second, equally important task. Call it Job 1b: enabling the ongoing engagement and everyday progress of the people in the trenches of your organization who strive to execute that strategy. A multiyear research project whose results we described in our recent book, *The Progress Principle*, found that of all the events that can deeply engage people in their jobs, the single most important is making progress in meaningful work.

The pursuit and satisfaction of meaning is not one of many things to cover—instead, it is the primary one. As Amabile and Kramer also point out,

> People are more creative, productive, committed, and collegial in their jobs when they have positive inner work lives. But it's not just any sort of progress in work that matters. The first, and fundamental, requirement is that the work be meaningful to the people.

While we like this article by Amabile and Kramer, it also—like so many other piece that attempt to engage with this topic—falls short in a disappointing way. At the end of the article, although the problem has been satisfactorily identified, no worthwhile solution is offered. We read only that

> As an executive, you are in a better position than anyone to identify and articulate the higher purpose of what people do within your organization. Make that purpose real, support its achievement through consistent everyday actions, and you will create the meaning that motivates people toward greatness. Along the way, you may find greater meaning in your own work as a leader (Amabile and Kramer, 2012).

The real answer is far more complex and nuanced than this, and there are many more steps to implement a successful change in a company.

Another recent article that caught our eye in this connection was by Jessica Amortegui in *Fast Company* (2014), where she notes,

> Increasing a sense of meaningfulness at work is one of the most potent—and underutilized—ways to increase productivity, engagement, and performance.
>
> . . .
>
> Consider the latest survey findings from the Energy Project, an engagement and performance firm that focuses on workplace fulfillment, as well as the recent *New York Times* story on why many hate their jobs. The survey, which reached more than 12,000 employees across a broad range of companies and industries, found that 50% lack a level of meaning and significance at work.

That is half the work force.

And the benefits of employees finding meaning at work are well known. As Amortegui (2014) also notes,

> employees who derive meaning from their work are more than three times as likely to stay with their organizations—the highest single impact of any other survey variable they tested. By this account, meaning trumps items related to learning and growth, connection to a company's mission, and even work-life balance. And the employees who have meaning don't just stick around longer. They also report 1.7 times higher job satisfaction, and are 1.4 times more engaged at work.

Amortegui goes on to say that: "Increasing a sense of meaningfulness at work is one of the most potent—and underutilized—ways to increase productivity, engagement, and performance."

The benefits of an engaged workforce seem to be clear both from research and from practice.

This raises the question, of course, that if the benefits of increasing a sense of meaning are so clear, then why is it not being more successfully pursued? If half of workers lack this thing that would improve their performance on so many levels, then why aren't we trying to give it to them?

This book will demonstrate that one answer is because there have been some fundamental flaws in the ways analysts and organizations have approached this issue. Many of the challenges relate to the fact that organizations reflect the biases of their cultural context. Yet we can learn from these mistakes and challenges. The rest of this book will demonstrate the value and wisdom of a recalibrated approach to establishing a meaningful workplace through the adoption and practice of service leadership in the best interests of both employees and the organizations that employ them.

SENSEMAKING, CALLING, AND MEANING WITHIN ORGANIZATIONS

Our approach to attaining meaning at work is rooted in the concept of "service leadership." Great companies focus on "serving"—both inside and outside their organizations. Literally, to serve means to perform duties to another. That other can be a person or an organization. In a workplace, a "service mindset" is typically understood to be driven by a strong underlying sense of purpose. In other words, there is purpose behind the corporation's vision and mission.

At the same time it establishes purpose, an organization must, in turn, serve its own employees. How does it do that? Succinctly, organizations need to serve their employees by providing them with the opportunity to pursue "whole and integrated meaning" within a corporate context. By serving its workers in this way, the organization will be more effective in serving both itself and its clients. **Service leadership** is a corporation's desire both to serve

its employees by facilitating their individual pursuit of ɪ
integrated meaning, and to have employees correspondingly sċ
outsiders more effectively through this pursuit of meaning.

It should be noted that this approach is distinct from the commonly used term "servant leadership." The concept of servant leadership has existed in many times and places, but the name was originally coined by Robert K. Greenleaf in "The Servant as Leader," an essay first published in 1970. In that essay, Greenleaf explained that the servant-leader is servant first and leads through example. The servant-leader shares power, puts the needs of others first, and helps people develop and perform as effectively as they possibly can.

Service leadership is distinct from servant leadership. Where "servant" puts the onus on the *person*, "service" focuses on the *process* and the *interaction* within the organization. We use the term service leadership to encapsulate the overall ethos of the organization, which addresses sensemaking, calling, and meaning for individuals.

At its core, service leadership addresses a primary challenge of the workplace: what will motivate an organization's employees to be fully engaged in the corporate purpose?

We know that individuals will attempt to make sense of their work environment in relation to their own framework of meaning and purpose. At times, their own personal frameworks may be different from the organization's framework. This lack of alignment presents a significant challenge. The organization, ideally driven by a clear purpose, attempts to fully engage and mobilize its workers in that same mission in order to get individuals pulling toward the same goal. You're up against a lot! Workers have already spent years—in some cases, decades—thinking about their identity, the meaning of their lives, and what they find meaningful. The lone worker has a significant challenge! How does an individual definition of meaning, calling, and happiness (which may already be developed and honed in particular directions) come to exist successfully within an organizational context?

One way to begin to formulate an answer to this question is to examine the meaning of the term **sensemaking.** In its simplest form, sensemaking is the process by which people give meaning to experience. Sensemaking has been defined as "an elegant, subtle, and richly descriptive body of thinking about human perception, cognition, and action, as well as social interaction, institutional reproduction and change, and human agency" (McNamara, 2015). Another definition: "Sensemaking is the process through which people work to understand issues or events that are novel, ambiguous, confusing, or in some other way violate expectations" (Maitlis and Christianson, 2014).

However you define it, sensemaking has implications for how to approach organizational leadership. Extensive empirical research shows that that many view sensemaking through the lens of a personal quest for calling. Individuals want to feel that their lives matter, that there is some greater purpose to their life. This leads them to try to identify their calling and meaning.

These ideas are strongly connected to a word we haven't used yet—happiness. It can be hard to engage with the concept of happiness because it can seem so general, all-encompassing, and over-reaching. John F. Schumaker, a clinical psychologist, has noted that "The quest for happiness has become nothing short of a cultural obsession . . . Personal happiness as an end in itself that transcends all other values is quite a recent development" (Schumaker, 2007).

But when it comes to happiness, those who research it consistently find that the single most effective step people can take to increase it is to turn their attention outward and focus on serving and helping other people. Happily, in attempting to increase the happiness of others, subjects will end up increasing their own.

As Schumaker notes, "One of the best means of finding happiness is to become absorbed into a cause greater than oneself" (ibid., p. 286). In other words, happiness comes through finding meaning by serving others.

Organizations that understand this work to create a particular culture for employees that accepts and engages with the ways employees pursue happiness, calling, and meaning. Most employees want their work to be in sync with their inner selves, and in sync with their pursuit of meaning and happiness. This is particularly so with "millennials."[1] While the findings of this book work across generations, they seem particularly relevant to those entering the workforce today. The organizations with the most committed individuals are those that can help their employees live out their own inner callings. Service leadership within an organization works most effectively when the purpose of an organization aligns with the individual calling of its employees. That way, both are fulfilled simultaneously.

This book reviews in detail the nature of calling and relates it to sensemaking and purpose within an organizational context. It explores how companies can facilitate the callings of their employees. To date, there has been a gap between the ardent desire for calling by individuals and the ability or interest of companies to understand and deal with this desire.

The objective of this book is to help businesses identify a concept of service leadership that will engage workers with their sense of calling, and then give a practical framework to let them act on it.

A challenge for many workers is that they feel unable to pursue their sense of calling within their current work environment. As a result, they often experience an underlying sense that something is missing. We call this disconnect between the individual's interest in the pursuit of meaning and the company's failure to address this concern the "**meaning gap**." This gap affects the quality of work and the productivity and energy of employees and, ultimately, of companies, too.

Companies and their leaders are typically not adequately attuned to the desires and core motivations of their employees. This can

---

1   "Millennials" are the cohort born between 1982 and 2004.

have far-reaching negative consequences. But fortunately, the situation can be corrected if the company is willing to engage with a program of service leadership.

Service leadership creates a culture of service within their organizations. It is a means for company leaders to empower their employees and ultimately build a more effective organization. Service leadership embraces the notion of calling and sensemaking that leaders typically have for themselves and applies it to people throughout the organization.

The approach to service leadership recommended in this book is based on both extensive research and practice. This includes interviews and work with over three hundred companies and their founders or chief executives over the past decade. The companies come from five continents, different religious traditions, and various industries and are led by both women and men. Some are private and others are publicly listed companies. But the crucial common thread is the benefit that service leadership can have for all of these organizations.

THE OUTLINE OF THE ARGUMENT

The objective of this book is to introduce you to service leadership in a clear, easy-to-understand way, and as expeditiously as possible. With that approach in mind, what follows is an outline of the core ideas and precepts of service leadership. You can read them over now and expect that they will be explored in greater detail later on in the book.

- Managing employees is managing people. The majority of people are spiritual, whether in a formal (religious) or informal manner. Spirituality matters to employees.
- Companies desire to have happy, motivated, content employees. We know this is true because companies demonstrably attempt to accommodate their needs

(i.e., job satisfaction, interest in community, desire for relationship).

- Companies can reach these goals for employees by focusing on meaning in the workplace.
- The likelihood or ability of individuals to achieve meaning depends upon the prevalence of "**meaning determinants**" in the workplace, which can include elements such as purpose, mastery of work, and autonomy.
- These meaning determinants vary according to the organizational context, which can include: type of industry, nature of organization (professional firms of lawyers, accountants, etc.), organizational structure (bureaucratic/governmental versus entrepreneurial), and leadership role (senior or junior).
- In order to understand how companies can cross the line by delving into meaning in the wrong way, we can distinguish three levels of meaning for individuals that we together refer to as the "**meaning hierarchy**": ultimate meaning, meaning at work, and meaningful activity.
- Companies can address meaning determinants in various ways such as the advancement of the corporate culture, the promotion of "values," or through training in specific value-systems.
- Companies often promote their corporate culture without pausing to consider how it may—or may not—connect with an employee's deeply held values and worldview (which may be different from the company's). We call this "**meaning creep**."
- Meaning creep is often facilitated by the fact that company leaders doubt the presence of religion as an important motivating factor in the lives of employees, having accepted the societal notion that the removal of

religion from the public square is equated with removal from the minds and hearts of employees ("**religion doubt**").

- Too often, companies employ a one-dimensional, uniform approach to advancing a particular view of meaning. They assume that there is a "**meaning vacuum**"—in other words, a misguided notion that employees have not independently constructed their own forms of meaning, whether or not through organized religion.

- Companies do not recognize or promote the concept of "**meaning diversity**," which is a recognition and acceptance of different approaches—religious, spiritual, or otherwise—regarding meaning at work. These companies fail to understand what we call the "**meaning spectrum**."

- An individual's pursuit of meaning is often couched in terms of personal purpose or "calling," a concept that has deep roots in Western thought. (The conventional concept of calling involves a "caller," such as an external or divine source.)

- While the concept of calling arose in a particular religious context, it is now commonly used and essentially devoid of religious connotations. (The contemporary concept of calling can be based on an internal sense of direction.)

- Companies need a better awareness of how individuals make sense of life and pursue calling, and this awareness needs to be reflected in their methods of dealing with employees.

- If they fail to understand calling, companies will likely work counter to their own purposes by trying to establish uniformity among employees in the realms of sensemaking and meaning.

- Companies may mistakenly believe that adopting language or concepts that have arisen from areas like religion will make a religious statement about their organization, or give it a religious identity. This is not the case.

- Companies generally make four faulty assumptions about workers and meaning:
  - First, they assume everyone just wants to be happy—but defines happiness primarily in terms of monetary rewards. In fact, there are many people who want to live lives of rich meaning and significance free from self-directed indulgence.
  - Second, if they discuss meaning at all, they assume they can do so without reference to any of the related spiritual wisdom accumulated over thousands of years.[2]
  - Third, they do not make the basic connection that a discussion about meaning at work needs to be related to a discussion about meaning of life.
  - Fourth, they do not distinguish levels of meaning. As a result, lesser forms of meaning—such as the value of relationships in the workplace—are equated as leading to meaning at work.
- "**Meaning chill**" describes an atmosphere in which any discussion with religious connection or overtones is viewed inappropriate.
- Companies act inappropriately when they presume that they can reshape the "core identity" of an employee. This approach can be an affront to employees.
- The inability to understand employees as meaning-seeking individuals has ramifications for the scope and meaning of corporate culture, and for vision and mission statements.
- Today, the common corporate approach to workplace culture and meaningfulness does not reflect service

---

2   See, for example, Ted Malloch's *Spiritual Enterprise*.

leadership, and it is not in the service of the well-being
and best interests of employees—but ultimately the
opposite.

- If companies focused on serving individuals to enable
  them to pursue their own sense of meaning, rather than
  meanings advanced by the company, they would realize a
  more positive outcome.
- Implementing a service leadership approach should have
  the outcome of employees being more motivated, and
  for longer periods of time, due to increased alignment of
  meaning with their job function.
- The company leads by serving its employees through
  creating an environment where the employees' pursuit
  of meaning is respected and recognized, enabling them
  to flourish to their utmost at the company. This creates
  "meaning space" for employees.
- Service leadership is good for a company! Studies show
  that individuals who believe that their work ties in with
  their calling or meaning and purpose are better and more
  contented employees. They work better and harder, and
  feel more deeply rewarded.
- Service leadership respects an employee's maturity and
  life choices. It works to provide meaning as they have
  defined it.
- Service leadership should then, ultimately, produce
  better outcomes for outsiders who work with the
  company; the culture of a company and the healthiness
  of an organization are typically evident to outsiders or
  stakeholders.
- Life and work issues are often coupled for employees, and
  service leadership provides a suitable balance of life and
  work. Service leadership deals with a person's whole and
  integrated life. This produces optimal outcomes for both
  the company and the employee.

CHAPTER 2

ORGANIZATIONAL AND PERSONAL DISCONNECT

Issues and challenges: the corporate disconnect

Companies and "meaning creep"

Companies and "the line of meaning"

John Rawls and Overlapping Consensus

ISSUES AND CHALLENGES: THE CORPORATE DISCONNECT

Deep-seated influences in Western culture color and shape the mindset we use when approaching areas thought to have a religious aspect. Consider the example of a public institution like the university. It can provide a good indicator of how religion and faith are viewed within modern Western society.

American philosopher John Cobb has described mainstream academia as trapped in the mechanistic worldview of René Descartes (1596–1650), which leaves no room for meaning or purpose. In Canada, also according to Cobb, students on the campuses of state-funded universities view their environment as "ruthlessly secular"; they believe that talking about spirituality would not be well received and are frightened to express their religious beliefs. With the rise of pluralism and relativism, there is less talk of truth and more of tolerance, which is often held up as a much higher value. Present academic ideology in turn impacts how companies approach their employees.

Many companies have lately adjusted their corporate culture to suit workers coming from the academic climate described above. This is especially true at large companies, at publicly held companies, and in government. These organizations stay vigilant in their pursuit of "political correctness," and this has extended to being careful never to endorse anything with a religious dimension. As Izzo and Klein put it. "The everyday language of business has fenced out the soul, the spiritual and the sacred." Many companies still operate as if religion and spirituality were either nonexistent or a niche phenomenon. This is a critically faulty assumption and can bring serious negative consequences. Too often, companies fail to distinguish between spirituality falling out of the public sphere and spirituality failing to exist any longer at all.

Other authors have recognized this misstep. For example, in his book *Drive*, business author Daniel Pink argues that "It is in our nature to seek purpose. But that nature is now being revealed and expressed on a scale that is demographically unprecedented and, until recently, scarcely imaginable. The consequences could rejuvenate our businesses and remake our world."

We agree that the impact on business could be significant. It is erroneous to suggest, however, that this "nature is [just] now being revealed." There has been a long tradition of purpose seeking in a variety of fields. In the same work, Pink also notes that "The science shows that the secret to high performance isn't our biological drive or our reward-and-punishment drive, but our third drive—our deep-seated desire to direct our own lives, to extend and expand our abilities, and to make a contribution." Again, this is important, but it's actually old news. What Pink and others miss so spectacularly is the link between purpose seeking and the institutions that have existed for thousands of years as an organized and systematic way of seeking purpose. That is: religion.

Why is Pink so coy about it? It is interesting to note that there is not a single reference in his book's index to "calling," "meaning," "religion," or "spirituality." This appears, in a book that ostensibly focuses on what drives human behavior and allows people to find purpose.

Elsewhere in his book, Pink notes that "So, in the end, repairing the mismatch and bringing our understanding of motivation into the twenty-first century is more than an essential move for business. It's an affirmation of our humanity." We would say this sounds like an affirmation of our nature—which we seek to serve in pursuit of a cause greater than ourselves.

In the UK, an innovation hub known as the Big Innovation Centre issued *The Purposeful Company Policy Report* in February 2017, which noted that "companies with a declared purpose, adhered to by their leadership teams and well understood by their stake holders, perform better on key metrics over time than their less purposeful peers."

What is "purpose"? The Report went on to explain that "A purposeful company is inspired by a clear role in the world that offers it a reason for being—its purpose. Purpose informs its existence, determines its goals, values and strategy, and is embedded in culture and practice." The Report also explains that "purposeful companies contribute meaningfully to human betterment and create long-term value for their stakeholders." One of the sets of stakeholders is employees. The Report notes that "Purposeful companies develop cultures based on trust and respect so that workplaces provide an opportunity for people to learn, contribute and thrive." The Report also notes that it is "particularly critical" to engage with employees so that they understand the company's strategy and adjust their expectations accordingly.

There is typically an assumption by companies—which is reflected in this Report—that companies, in the guise of Big Brother, will take apparently purposeless individuals and then motivate and inspire them to fulfill and comport with the company's sense of purpose. Yet companies are not generally spiritually inclusive. It is, perhaps, the final realm of prejudice and parochialism allowed and fostered by companies, in which a dominant narrative is presented. Companies do not promote a single ethnicity, sexuality, or gender— but they do reflect a single approach to spirituality, meaning, and purpose. They can do so explicitly or implicitly: explicitly by simply making religion and spirituality "off limits" for discussion at the office, and implicitly by not recognizing the religious elements that inform and enrich the lives of employees.

At most workplaces, the big fear is still proselytization; that a discussion of religion and spirituality could open a door to some religious people attempting to win others over to their way of thinking. This seems to create a "**meaning chill**" in which anything that smacks of religion must be zealously avoided. Perhaps there needs to be new and different language. There is a significant difference between having an environment of open dialogue about religious belief and promoting a particular belief system. The current climate is particularly troubling because meaning in life is ranked as an important topic for many employees, and, according to a Pew Survey in 2015, 85 percent of the world's population has religious attachments.

COMPANIES AND "MEANING CREEP"

Should companies be able to delve into the "personal space" that comprises an employee's sense of meaning? Should companies help employees set personal goals in furtherance of corporate objectives? It is telling that most business leaders would have trouble answering these questions quickly and decisively. These same leaders could align around the idea that helping employees with time management and organizational skills is clearly acceptable but would blanche at company involvement in developing life goals as they relate to ultimate meaning.

It's time that we asked precisely how a company's approach to advancing corporate values impinges on a person's pursuit of meaning, and why assisting with deeper, more meaningful goals is not considered appropriate.

Meaning Determinants

We have identified six meaning determinants that work together as the framework for a person's search for meaning. By understanding these determinants, organizations can engage appropriately and effectively with employees on a variety of levels. Let's begin by reviewing each of them in turn.

First, the employee has identified a source of spirituality in his or her life (Yahweh, Jesus Christ, Allah, a god or gods, or even just a spiritual feeling). This deity or spiritual feeling may be communicated with at a specific location (church, synagogue, temple, etc.) or at multiple locations.

Second, the employee engages on some level with a study of a source document in connection to the pursuit of meaning (e.g., the Bible, the Torah, the Koran).

Third, the employee may attend regular gatherings with others spiritually like-minded individuals.

Fourth, the employee seeks an alignment of life goals, and purpose, with the source of their meaning.

Fifth, in the employee's perspective, the meaning framework of his or her life is something that work fits into.

Sixth, because of this established framework, the employee resists when the company they work for attempts to supplant or overshadow his or her personal pursuit of meaning; but the employee responds positively when the company instead looks to contribute to it.

This meaning framework hopefully provides an outline of the "backbone" of meaning for most workers and can help companies understand how to navigate around it. We're not aware of any company that has developed an in-depth approach to recognizing and working with the concept of meaning that also recognizes an employee's own nuanced approach to meaning. To the contrary, if they engage at all, companies typically infringe upon the worker's established meaning framework.

In order to understand how companies can cross the line by delving into meaning in the wrong way, we can distinguish three levels of meaning for individuals. We'll refer to these three together as the "**meaning hierarchy**."

The first level of this hierarchy is "**ultimate meaning**"—that is to say, meaning in the big picture. This level of meaning attempts to address what most people see as the ultimate question: what is the point of my life? Few people would expect a company to answer this most fundamental question for them—and, in fact, few companies try to. But by neglecting entirely that most employees are interested in this question on some level, companies can unknowingly engage in missteps that make employees feel stifled and constrained in their attempts to answer this question.

The second level of the hierarchy is **"meaning at work."** This refers to the search for meaning in the context of one single aspect of life. People are more likely, though not always, willing to accommodate a company's initiative regarding this single aspect of meaning as it relates to work, and with connecting ideas such as what type of person they are, and what their goals and motivations are. At that same time, there will always be a few employees who are uncomfortable with any infringement into this area. People will have different tolerance levels. This is okay and should be expected.

The third level of the hierarchy is **"meaningful activity,"** which relates to moments or experiences that are valuable in a non-systematic and unstructured way. Most companies can provide much in the way of meaningful activity. For example, through a company's products or services, an employee can assist a particular person on a particular day. The relationships between employees in the workplace can also be a source of meaning. Companies need to understand this meaning hierarchy. Companies can delve into meaningful activity, and with a careful approach they can engage in meaning at work, but they should always be careful not impinge on the pursuit of ultimate meaning.

When we're discussing meaning, it's also important to note that there are multiple sources of meaning. These sources include faith, family, friends, hobbies, sport, and work, to name but a few. Yet rarely does one of these, however important, fulfill and constitute all meaning in a person's life. Research confirms that people look to multiple sources of meaning in life (reported in McGrath 2015, p. 154). Businesses, then, would do well to realize that regardless of how important they would like work to become in the minds of employees, there will always be competing sources of meaning. Companies do better when they appreciate this fact rather than when they try to force disproportionate emphasis on work and make it the dominant source of meaning—and, especially not, something that smacks of ultimate meaning.

There is a subtle but important distinction to be noted regarding how companies approach meaningfulness in work. Companies face several challenges in their approach to employee engagement when it overlaps with meaning and purpose. First, employees are—and often should be—skeptical when an employer talks about meaning, because they suspect that the company likely has ulterior motives (to make employees more productive, for example). Second, in pushing an approach to meaning, the company is offering long-term solutions within the context of what may potentially be a short-term or indeterminate relationship. Third, from the perspective of most workers, while the company is probably an expert in its business (product), the employee has no reason to think it is an expert when it comes to the pursuit of meaning. So, why should an employee simply accept a company's proffering of a meaning construct? Fourth, company culture drives uniformity, but people want a degree of individuality. And fifth, a company may not be willing to accept alternative sources of the pursuit of meaning.

Employees are right to resist the "meaning creep" that happens when companies encroach too far into the personal realm, especially since employment is increasingly for shorter time periods and rarely for life, and people will have a variety of jobs during their lifetimes.

Most companies have not fully grasped the nature of religion and spirituality in society and how it exists through people in the workplace. There are three aspects of present society that create a phenomenon we call "**religion doubt**" within society and the workplace. The first aspect is secularization, which entails the removal of the trappings of religion as much as is practicable from the state and the public square. Secularization has led to the dismissal and disregard of religious belief. Secularists assume that society will outgrow religion or that it will wither away. Now many businesses assume this, too. The second aspect is what we call a kind of religious privatization. People can have religious beliefs—they just can't voice them publicly. They must be kept private. For example, a person who has views regarding abortion or sexual morality informed by his or her religious convictions increasingly feels that these views cannot be publicly articulated. And although these religious beliefs get pushed out from the public arena, the reality is that people still hold them and they act accordingly in terms of their motivations and priorities. Companies need to understand this. The third factor leading to religion doubt is the characterization of proselytization as offensive and inappropriate. Talking about a religion in any context can raise alarm—it is routinely viewed as a taboo subject. It makes people protest that someone is trying to "jam religion down their throat"!

These three aspects of religion in society contribute to the overriding feeling now prevalent across our society that religion is best kept out of the public square. However, greatly restricting the spheres in which a discussion of religion—that is, an organized pursuit of meaning—is allowed to take place does not mean it no longer exists.

Companies too often act as if this "privatized" religion means there is a vacuum to fill in the minds and lives of employees. We call this the "**meaning vacuum**." It is presumptuous to think that individuals have not satisfactorily pursued meaning in the past and that now that they have joined a particular company, the company can simply do it for them—and that companies may then promote their own concept of meaning and significance (their ethos) to their employees as the uniform way to have meaning (and then significance). This promotion usually ties into an explicit or implicit "agenda" of the company and is typically intended to serve the employees rather than to serve the company. This is unfortunate and inappropriate. This is not service leadership.

Many companies that do this have their hearts in the right places. It can be admirable that a company is trying to meet their workers for meaning, particularly as work consumes the bulk of the employees' waking hours and much of their intellectual energy. But the company needs to take the step of defining the boundaries of its culture, tied into effectiveness, and anything falling outside that scope should be left to the individual. For example, does the company allow, acknowledge, or encourage time for religious observance—evenings, weekdays, and holy days—and the wearing of religious garb?[3] To what extent is accommodation accepted? Individuals typically pursue meaning at work in relation to how they pursue meaning in their lives. The core of service leadership is that a company provides a more open platform for meaning and a safe environment in which to pursue it. The company must also be meticulously aware of the differences between things they may promote that relate to the realm of the pursuit of meaning and those that are merely meaningful activities within the realm of enjoyment or pleasure.

When it comes to the search for meaning, a company needs to accept diversity, rather than stifle it. An evangelical Christian, a devout Muslim, and an Orthodox Jew should all be able to live their calling and feel comfortable within the same company. They should feel that they are free to practice their faiths, and that the company is supportive of this. They can also accept the full ethos of the company at the same time. In this connection, companies should embrace "**meaning diversity**." Unfortunately, too few do.

Instead, companies often disregard the value of established faith traditions—rooted in thousands of years of history—and instead attempt to provide ultimate meaning to employees based on a track record of their own short experience in the pursuit of meaning in the workplace. In a nutshell, companies can provide job satisfaction, fun and games, and socializing, but they should not have programs based on a set philosophy that delves into the ultimate meaning of life. That crosses the line.

COMPANIES AND "THE LINE OF MEANING"

Where is the "**line of meaning**," and when is that line crossed? Organized systems for the pursuit of meaning, such as specific

---

3   This is particularly relevant in the European context, where countries such as France are challenging the wearing of the hijab in public settings.

religious faiths, comprise not just theology and concepts of God or divinity, but also practical applications for living. Faiths require not only belief, but also acting on them, practicing them, especially in the face of the ever-present charge of hypocrisy. Companies need to tread between not delving into ultimate meaning and being careful with respect to meaning at work. When they dismiss, avoid, or disregard the pursuit of meaning by individuals through religious channels, they make an all-too-common misstep.

Companies typically adopt an exclusionary approach to meaning in the workplace and instead advance a singular corporate culture to fill that void. While it's true that *some* employees may be a complete tabula rasa, those are in the minority. Our question becomes how, then, to deal with the majority? Even within the majority, there will be a diversity of views and practices. Some people are "institutionally" religious. They are unable to do weekend retreats, divulge to strangers, or talk about their belief systems in detail, especially when the broader world may largely dismiss or even mock their beliefs. A company should understand where workers may be coming from when it comes to these activities. A worker who is uncomfortable engaging with colleagues when it comes to his or her faith is not necessarily resistant to a religious search for meaning. In fact, the opposite may be true in a very powerful way.

This book is about service leadership and how a company can adopt the principles of service leadership to become a more effective organization. We believe that companies can achieve a competitive advantage through service leadership: attracting and retaining employees; creating a positive work environment; and hiring more effective employees. We will now delve further into how sensemaking individuals—employees—approach their pursuits of meaning.

JOHN RAWLS AND OVERLAPPING CONSENSUS

When it comes to effective engagement with employee mindsets regarding religion and meaning, there is some precedence in philosophical thinking.

The American moral and political philosopher John Rawls—in *A Theory of Justice* (1999)—coined the term "overlapping consensus" to refer to how supporters of different doctrines can agree on particular principles of justice that underwrite a political community's basic social institutions. Just as Rawls speaks of doctrines, we refer to meaning frameworks. The applicability to our discussion is that both employers and employees can have an overlapping consensus on the importance of meaning at work, yet they have different concepts of how that meaning is achieved.

Rawls explains that an overlapping consensus on principles can occur despite "considerable differences in citizens' conceptions of justice provided that these conceptions lead to similar political judgments." Different groups are able to achieve consensus in part by refraining from political/public disputes over fundamental (e.g., metaphysical) arguments on religion and philosophy. Rawls thinks that the existence of an overlapping consensus on conceptions of justice among major social groups holding differing—yet reasonable—comprehensive doctrines is a necessary and distinctive characteristic of classically liberal societies.

Rawls also believes that the overlapping consensus on principles of justice is itself a moral conception and is supported by moral reasoning. Again, there is an interesting parallel with our approach, but there are clear differences. Employers and employees can have overlapping consensuses on the value of meaning at work but still have different ways of approaching it. We are not suggesting a Rawlsian theory of justice and can see the limitations of his philosophical arguments. Even so, his ideas on the overlapping of doctrines directly inform our discussion of how best to engage with employees and find commonalities in a search for meaning.

In the next chapter, we will build on these ideas and look at how individuals engage in sensemaking in the context of spirituality and religion.

CHAPTER 3

SENSEMAKING FOR INDIVIDUALS: THE CONTEXT OF RELIGION AND SPIRITUALITY

Rodney Stark: a sociologist's view

Niall Ferguson: an historian's view

Five trends in spirituality relevant to the workplace

Conclusion

In Chapter 1, we described the notion of "service leadership" and introduced terms like sensemaking, calling, and meaning. We also outlined the critical role of service leadership in terms of its positive impact in an organization—providing a sense of meaning for employees, increasing engagement, and facilitating retention. In Chapter 2, we focused on the organizational and personal disconnects that can occur in understanding the pursuit of sensemaking, calling, and meaning in an organizational context. Our discussion in these first two chapters was based on fundamental premises— the most basic of these is that individuals are ultimately purpose-seeking individuals to whom the pursuit of meaning is fundamental to their life and contentment. A further fundamental premise is that the pursuit of sensemaking is most typically (and historically) channeled through religion and spirituality.

In this chapter, we will explore how individuals engage in sensemaking. We'll first examine spirituality in Western culture in terms of broad societal trends. In other words, we'll look at the context within which people engage in their individual discernment of meaning. Next, we will review the specific religious concept of calling, and the role it has played in Western culture (particularly in relation to capitalism and work ethic). We will then examine how the concept of calling has manifested itself in the present day in the ways individuals approach their work.

Employees join organizations as holistic and integrated individuals, who have previously engaged with the pursuit of meaning in their lives. The first step that will allow organizations to work effectively with individuals—and thus to engage in true service leadership—is to understand this about them. A central question we'll examine in this chapter is: Do religion and spirituality still qualify as "relevant" in our society today, and do they still make significant impacts on individuals?

At this moment in history, the worldview of many is that religion is in irreversible decline, and that, each day, the religious sphere becomes less and less relevant. The facts are different. Though the prevalence of religion in culture may have receded momentarily in some Western countries, one should not conclude that this constitutes 1.) an irreversible trend, or 2.) a trend that applies to the entire world. China, for example, is an interesting reference point. A conservative guess, back in 2009, was that there are at least 65 million Protestants and 12 million Catholics in China, and that this number is growing (Micklethwait and Wooldridge, 2009, p. 4). The Chinese see positive aspects to an open engagement with the religious aspects of life and have no compunction about acknowledging this. A contemporary Chinese government economist, Zhao Xiao, has written a widely circulated essay that argues that the key to America's commercial success is not its natural resources, its financial system, or its technology, but its churches (ibid., p. 8). Perhaps as a consequence of this view, the Chinese have been joining the Christian church with enthusiasm because they view it as an enlightened and rewarding step to take. A representative Chinese view is that, "In Europe the church is old. Here [in China] it is modern. Religion is a sign of higher ideals and progress. Spiritual wealth and material wealth go together" (ibid., p. 9). The Christian church in China is just one example, but it's a big and powerful one. It should serve as a reminder that the recession of religion in public spheres in places like Europe and the United States is not necessarily indicative of a worldwide trend.

RODNEY STARK: A SOCIOLOGIST'S VIEW

An important contributor to the sociology of religion on a global scale is Rodney Stark, presently professor at Baylor University in Texas. He has published widely on topics related to sociology, often debunking widely held views. His contrarian views are substantiated by detailed research. One example is Stark's writings as they relate to the role of religion and spirituality in the West and globally. Stark makes the case that even though organized religion seems less prominent in the West, we're more interested than ever in the core ideas it deals with—namely, spirituality and meaning. As he writes in *The Triumph of Faith: Why The World is More Religious Than Ever*: "And what do the data tell us? Quite simply, that a massive religious awakening is taking place around the world" (Stark, 2015, p. 2). Stark also notes that strict atheism still makes up only a very small percentage of the world's faith perspectives, usually fewer than 5 percent (ibid., p. 3).

For too many, there is still a perception that unless faith comes in a neat box one can tick off—such as "Catholic" or "Jewish"—then that faith must not exist. Faiths themselves have also behaved, in recent years, in ways that have led to an apparent diminishing (that may not actually exist). Protestantism, for example, has a built-in fragmentation dynamic, an ever-present splitting, a stress on individualism, and a high degree of privatization.

To begin to access the very real and very strong current of religion and spirituality that still flows in Western culture—and is still the predominant source of the pursuit of meaning—we need to rethink our definitional approach. Our discussion cannot be restricted by institutional boundaries; we need to take a "big tent" approach. For a proper analysis of the situation, as Stark explains, we need to "distinguish between religion and mere supernaturalism. It also will be useful to distinguish between churched and unchurched religions and supernaturalisms" (Stark, 2015, p. 7). Stark's definitions are as follows: "Supernatural" refers to "forces or entities beyond or outside nature and having the capacity to suspend, alter, or ignore physical forces" (ibid.). One example is astrology. "Religion" is "a form of supernaturalism that postulates the existence of gods, conceived of as supernatural beings having consciousness and desires" (ibid.). "Churched religions" are those that "consist of relatively stable, organized congregations of lay members who acknowledge a specific religious creed" (ibid.). Stark also explains that "A creed is a set of beliefs to which all members of a religious group are expected to assent, and those who participate in churched religions are expected to do so regularly and exclusively" (ibid.). Stark further notes, "Both unchurched religions and unchurched supernaturalism lack organized congregations and usually lack a creed" (ibid.). In short, though persons falling into these categories may seem dissimilar, they are all engaging with spirituality and the search for meaning (in ways that would have traditionally been called "religious"). This has startling and powerful implications for business organizations, especially international ones. The chief point is that the world is not becoming more secular and organizations should not be doing their planning on that faulty implicit premise. Despite the high profile of strident atheists such as Richard Dawkins, author of *The Selfish Gene* (1976) and *The God Delusion* (2006), it is still the case that "In most of the world, atheists make up only tiny percentages of the population" (Stark, 2015, p. 31).

Stark concludes that, contrary to the impressions of many, a great resurgence of interest in religion and spirituality is taking place. Stark puts it plainly: "The world is religious. The one exception is Western Europe" (ibid., p. 37). He further makes the sanguine observation that "Church attendance may be low in Europe, but unconventional supernaturalism is thriving" (ibid., p. 45). One reason is that the American combination of modernity and religion is compelling—not just in China, but throughout much of Asia, Africa, Arabia, and Latin America (as noted by Micklethwait and Wooldridge, in their book *God is Back*, 2009, p. 12). In most cases, a growth of faith is seen to correspond with a growth in prosperity. This has been called a "theotropic beast," which Micklethwait and Wooldridge describe thusly: "given the option a person is inclined to believe in God because religion can increase material well being along with spiritual ways" (ibid., p. 16).

In fact, one reason for the decline in religious service attendance and religious identification in the West may be that this sense of connection between religion and success, competition, and capitalism has been lost.

According to Stark: "the more religious competition there is within a society, the higher the overall level of individual religious participation" (Stark, 2015, p. 56). In Europe, churches still remain divorced from the idea that religion can respond to or create worldly success. Stark further notes, "religious groups [that] sustain an image of an active God who makes moral demands will enjoy substantial competitive advantages over groups that present God as a psychological construct or an impersonal 'higher power'" (ibid.).

This belief obviously has significant implications for businesses seeking to understand and motivate employees.

Another reason for the chilling of religion in Western culture is that religion has been characterized as something for the uneducated masses (that they will essentially grow out of it over time). Sometimes pundits on television speak as if they believe religious people simply believe without reflection. This is not so.

Instead, people are motivated to continue engaging with spirituality and religion by an underlying sense that there is a design and purpose to the universe, that there must be a creator, and that they want the blessings of that creator. Stark explains that "the supernatural is a plausible source of many things humans greatly desire, some of which are otherwise unattainable" (ibid., p. 205).

Despite this, businesses almost never attempt to engage with a careful and nuanced understanding of spirituality and meaning seeking among employees. Nor do they stop to ask how this engagement might make them more effective. No. Instead, in this sphere, business organizations seem content to follow rather than to lead. They are content to reflect society's attitudes, and leave it at that. This represents a missed opportunity.

Any honest, serious survey of contemporary spirituality and religion concludes empirically that religion is thriving in many parts of the world, and that everyone is still interested in finding meaning in their lives. Every business must deal with the reality of this environment, because people in society end up being employees in organizations. There's great evidence that people still believe, and that they still want to believe.

Again, we need to distinguish Europe from the rest of the world. Stark explains that

> Only in parts of Europe are the churches still rather empty, but this is not the reliable sign of secularization it has long been said to be; it is, rather, a sign of lazy clergy and unsuitable established religions. As has been said, Europe is a continent of "believing non-belongers" (Stark, 2015, p. 212).

Those in organizations who are not religious may ask why religion endures. Stark notes that "People want to know why the universe exists, not that it exists for no reason, and they don't want their lives to be pointless. Only religion provides credible and satisfactory answers to the great existential questions" (ibid.). People still want to know the purpose to their lives, and how it connects to the work that they do. The bottom line is that this is a person's search for meaning, expressed formally or otherwise, and is something that organizations need to heed and engage with. It is not going away.

NIALL FERGUSON: AN HISTORIAN'S VIEW

So, present-day religion and spirituality are growing in much of the world, and though a pall may have been cast over them in the West, they are still very important to almost everyone. Our understanding of the intractable nature of faith can be bolstered even further by taking an historical view. Religion and spirituality are part of an historical preoccupation with the pursuit of meaning and are intertwined with all of Western history.

Virtually nobody would dispute the pervasive influence of religion—primarily Christianity in its various forms—as a shaping influence on Western thought and culture. In the post-World War II era—though it still may be very important and culturally dominant—we seem to no longer like the fact that it is. Religion is constantly discredited, disdained, and devalued. The great churches gracing the centers of many European cities are viewed as monuments to the past, to backwards thinking, and to ignorance. They are often converted to museums or used for other purposes. Just one example is the Oude Kerk, an historic church in Amsterdam open to visitors and located in the middle of what is now the red light district. The Oude Kerk is the oldest parish church in the city and was originally built in the 1300s. It was expanded over the years to its present form, which dates from the 18th century. Now the Oude Kerk houses one of the Netherland's youngest art institutions. Visitors can even visit a café in the former sacristy.

What has been the role of religion in the West? Further, does it provide some underpinnings of the nature of Western culture to this very day? We will focus in this brief section on the work of Niall Ferguson. He is a prominent historian with appointments at both Harvard and Stanford and a slew of awards for both his writing and documentary productions. Ferguson has gained a wide audience due to his exceptional ability to seize grand themes and communicate his perspective—typically informed and unique—to a wide audience. Recently, he has used his powers to highlight the role of religion in the development and shaping of Western civilization. One of Ferguson's books is particularly relevant for our discussion, as it provides a backdrop as to how a concept of calling—long embedded in the Christian faith—gained such wide currency in Western society and, through its historical preeminence, to other societies, too. In *Civilization: The West and the Rest* (2011), Ferguson notes that the rise of the West "is, quite simply, the pre-eminent historical phenomenon of the second half of the second millennium after Christ" (p. 18).

Ferguson notes that the West is distinguished from "the Rest" by six crucial features that are worth noting. First, there was competition: Europe was politically fragmented and within each monarchy or republic there were multiple competing corporate entities. Second, science: all the major seventeenth-century breakthroughs in mathematics, astronomy, physics, chemistry, and biology happened in Western Europe. Third, the importance of property rights: the rule of law and representative government, based on private property rights and the representation of property-owners in elected legislatures. Fourth, medicine: nearly all major nineteenth- and twentieth-century breakthroughs in healthcare were made by Western Europeans and North Americans. Fifth, the West has a consumer society: the Industrial Revolution took place where there was both a supply of productivity-enhancing technologies and a demand for more, better, and cheaper goods. The sixth feature that Ferguson believes contributes to the ascendency of the West ties in with the thrust of this book. This feature is the "work ethic."

Ferguson argues that "Westerners were the first people in the world to combine more extensive and intensive labor with higher savings rates, permitting sustained capital accumulation" (Ferguson, 2011, p. 17). Where did this come from? How did it come about? Ferguson explains that the origins of the "work ethic" lie in faith. As he puts it, "Protestantism, rather, the peculiar ethic of hard work and thrift, was a key advantage over the rest of the world" (Ferguson, 2011, p. 259). He notes that Max Weber's seminal book *The Protestant Ethic and the Spirit of Capitalism* "contains one of the most influential of all arguments about Western civilization: that its economic dynamism was an unintended consequence of the Protestant Reformation" (Ferguson, 2011, p. 261). While the Protestant work ethic and corresponding spirituality are not embraced now in the same way they may have been in previous generations, there has not necessarily been a decline in the use of spirituality as a guide for meaning and decision making. Ferguson notes that "From aromatherapy to *Zen and the Art of Motorcycle Maintenance*, the West today is awash with post-modern cults, none of which offers anything remotely as economically invigorating or socially cohesive as the old Protestant ethic" (ibid., p. 289).

Well-defined religions and traditions still exist, even if a strange bazaar of spirituality has grown in their midst. We need to now examine in greater detail the nature of spirituality and the context it provides for people seeking meaning in their lives. For inevitably they will bring that quest for meaning with them into the workplace.

FIVE TRENDS IN SPIRITUALITY RELEVANT TO THE WORKPLACE

While established, organized religious bodies and denominations are easy to identify, this is not the case with entities catering to spirituality. Religious organizations typically have historical traditions and an infrastructure, sometimes developed over hundreds of years, of church buildings, schools and universities, and head offices and staff. Religious organizations, whether denominations or parachurch entities, have established leaders and teams to implement their vision and mission. But what of spirituality? It is a pervasive influence within and throughout society, which is more difficult to identify. So, to start, we need to define what is meant by spirituality.

Spirituality (in today's world) is generally defined as the pursuit of meaning in life through eclectic means, without the need for (or use of) an institutionalized infrastructure. While religion is also concerned with the pursuit of meaning in life, unlike spirituality, it typically accesses the support of an infrastructure and a set of institutions. Spirituality is a way of conducting one's life in relation to the pursuit of one or more of the meaning hierarch: meaningful activity, meaning at work, and ultimate meaning. Spirituality acts as a canopy under which the key influences of today's environment can be placed. It is no easy feat to define spirituality, however. Here is a comment from Phil Knight, Founder, NIKE, Inc., on his pursuit of meaning for youngsters embarking on their careers: "The harder you work, the better your Tao. And since no one has ever adequately defined Tao, I now try to go regularly to mass. I would tell them: Have faith in yourself, but also have faith in faith. Not faith as others define it. Faith as you define it. Faith as faith defines itself in your heart" (Knight, 382). This would be somewhat reflective of today's approach to spirituality.

We need to understand spirituality, and its rise, in order to fully understand the individuals who are seeking meaning within an organizational context. We can define spirituality as rooted in several societal trends that explain its diffuse nature: deinstitutionalization; secular humanism; postmodernism; the New Age movement; and the human potential movement. First, there has been a steady deinstitutionalization within Western society over the past fifty years.[4] There has been a movement toward personalized spirituality and a drift away from religion in an organized and institutionalized sense. The term "spirituality" now refers to a quest to discover the answers to the ultimate questions of life and meaning, but not through traditional and organized religion. Today's spirituality often appears to be a means of distilling the so-called positive elements of religion, but not taking on the obligations, creeds, and commitment.

This shift in the Western perception and interpretation of institutionalized religion can be traced back to around the year 1700. Since that time, effective public advocates have played a central role in bringing about a new spiritual outlook (Herrick, p. 250). In a sense, this is a means of sanitizing religion and applying it to various aspects of life, including work. This is no longer a marginalized undertaking. This is a realigned and recalibrated quest, reflected most clearly in the generation that is forming its values in today's environment. The values of the millennials are increasingly shaped by their desire to determine their own customized fulfillment and purpose in life. Individuals no longer as readily accept in an unquestioning way the dictates coming from an organizational hierarchy.

---

4   In the United States, The Gallup Institute polls individuals as to religions and spiritual impact in their lives (see Gallup and Jones, 2000). In Canada, Reginald W. Bibby has conducted a number of studies that document this trend; see, for example, *Restless Gods* (2002). See also discussion by Charles Taylor, *A Secular Age* (2007, p. 508).

Media and technology also play a role in this trend. Individuals can passively observe a church service and have virtually no demands made upon them. There is evidence that little in the way of demand (or, for that matter, immersion) results in scanty allegiance. The rise of television and other media is one reason for the fewer church attendees throughout North America and Europe over the past fifty years. But this declining interest in institutionalized religion does not mean that there are necessarily fewer individuals embracing spirituality.

The vast majority of people still strive to answer the basic question of ultimate meaning: "Why am I here?" Indeed, a number of important psychologists have included humankind's spiritual nature—the perennial quest for meaning—as part of their theories of human behavior. According to one source, recent data report that more than 80 percent of the world's population expresses some sort of religious affiliation.[5] And as one popular business writer, Jack Canfield, states, "At some level we all hunger for meaning in our lives. We need to feel at our core that we matter, and that we are making a difference" (p. 272). As a result, one aspect of our modern environment is that, while there is less interest in religion viewed as structures and institutions, there remains a strong interest in spirituality. As noted earlier, organizations ignore this at their peril.

Now let's compare and contrast by taking a look at secular humanism, and what we really mean when we use the term. The foundations of secular humanism date back to the ideas of classical Greek philosophers, such as the Stoics and Epicureans, and to Chinese Confucianism. Under classical secular humanism, human beings, rather than an external force (such as a god), were the source of solutions to problems. That's essentially what it meant. But from the 20th century on, scientists, philosophers, and progressive theologians began to organize in an effort to promote the humanist alternative to traditional faith-based worldviews. These early organizers

---

5   The Spiritual Nature of a Human Being.

classified humanism as essentially a nontheistic religion that would fulfill the human need for an ordered ethical/philosophical system to guide one's life—essentially, a form of spirituality without the supernatural. In the last thirty years, many who reject supernaturalism as a viable philosophical outlook have adopted the term "secular humanism" to describe their nonreligious (or even antireligious) stance. This perspective can be seen currently—in its most strident form—promulgated by the New Atheists, with Richard Dawkins chief among them.

Another influence is postmodernism. The term, of course, needs to be defined in relation to "modernism." Modernism arose in the latter half of the 19th century, in a period of technological progress and expanding global commerce. A new capitalist order was created, which included international competition, and this disrupted many established ways of living and doing business. As we shall see in a discussion of Max Weber in Chapter 4, the modern epoch of capitalism was a system of rational, rule-governed behavior, organized around a central motivation: the continuous accumulation of profit as an end in itself. In his book *The Protestant Ethic and the Spirit of Capitalism*, Weber calls modernity an "iron cage" of modernity "that drew an ever-tightening noose of impersonal, abstract, instrumental rationality around its victims, leading to the suppression of spontaneity, diversity and mystery." Coming, then, to postmodernism, one can start by saying many view it as a continuation of the processes of modernization, but with increasing intensity and scope. The result of this intensification has been to erode the stability of modernity and throw it into some confusion. The outcome, according to Stanley Grenz, a theologian, is that "The postmodern consciousness has abandoned the Enlightenment belief in inevitable progress. Post-moderns have not sustained the optimism that characterized previous generations" (Grenz, 13). As Grenz further explains, "Postmodernism . . . entails a rejection of the emphasis on rational discovery through the scientific method, which provided the intellectual foundation for the modern attempt to construct a better world"(Grenz, 12). With the corresponding breakdown of the overarching narrative, the resulting confusion has manifested itself in perspectives such as relativism and the soul being experientially based.

A fourth trend is the so-called New Age movement. This movement is one of the twentieth century's unique creations. It began in the 1960s, when a disenchantment with established institutions and with traditional Western religion led to an infatuation with Eastern religions. The corresponding New Age has been defined by J.P. Newport in *The New Age Movement and the Biblical Worldview* as "a spiritual movement seeking to transform individuals and society through mystical union with a dynamic cosmos. Its advocates hope to bring about a utopian era, a 'New Age' of harmony and progress that some say has already begun" (Newport, 1). The New Age is more frequently referred to as a "movement" than as a "religion" since it is decentralized and not organized like traditional religions. For example, there are no uniformly acknowledged leaders or facilities, and there is no hierarchy of the New Age upon which its adherents agree. One website states that the movement can be viewed as "a free-flowing spiritual movement—a network of believers and practitioners—where book publishers take the place of a central organization; seminars, conventions, books and informal groups replace of [*sic*] sermons and religious services."

A fifth trend, which is an offshoot of the New Age movement, is called the "human potential movement." This movement involves the adaptation of the New Age to small business, to entrepreneurs, and to corporations. It includes anything from seminars to training sessions to follow-up materials—that involve self-motivation and self-power. So-called "gurus" play a significant role in the human potential movement. These gurus are generally followed because of their charisma and professed expertise. Under the typical paradigm of this movement, to achieve maximum results, an individual must follow a series of exercises that are designed to confirm the individual's self-power. Examples range from Tony Robbins's "fire walk" to

Brian Tracy's Phoenix Seminars to forms of self-hypnosis. Most of the gurus in this movement are essentially professional speakers who can appear at hundreds of venues in a single year. Each speaking event typically involves heavy promotion of the guru's product line of tapes, books, and daily journals. Many proponents of the human potential movement focus on the importance of mind control and mastery. There are many elements of this movement that—while not explicitly religious—employ the language and ritual of religion. Certainly, one cannot attend one of the movement's events without sensing the "aroma" of the religious in the air.

CONCLUSION

Despite protestations to the contrary by many, religion and spirituality (now practiced under many names) remain an important aspect of people's lives and the most important way for them to develop their meaning frameworks. Rodney Stark's extensive research on the sociology of religion worldwide has amply demonstrated the widespread role of religion and the practice of spirituality. Niall Ferguson's insights, based on historical research, reveal the pivotal role of Christian faith embedded in Western culture that has subsequently impacted the world. We have highlighted the five trends of spirituality prevelant within society, though they are not always obvious due to their lack of institutional infrastructure. Companies need to become attuned to this dynamic of spirituality because individuals are holistic creatures; they bring their whole selves into the workplace.

In the next chapter, we will look in more detail at how workers construct their meaning frameworks. In particular, we'll examine the important role of calling as a central part of such sensemaking.

CHAPTER 4

SENSEMAKING FOR INDIVIDUALS: THE CONCEPT OF CALLING

Max Weber: the Protestant ethic and the spirit of capitalism

The Judeo-Christian approach to calling

John Maxwell: Christian-grounded calling

Dik and Duffy: calling in the mainstream

A Millennial's View: meaningful work

Conclusion

At the Vincent van Gogh Museum in Amsterdam, an exhibition panel explains that at the age of 27, van Gogh left his training for the Christian ministry to pursue his "true calling" as an artist. In other words, he pursued what he loved, what he had passion for. The message is that *this* is why his creative output was so wonderful. The use of the term "calling" is assumed to require no explanation. The term remains prevalent in our society today. Everyone knows what you mean when you use it.

Our discussion in the previous chapter provided a general context for spirituality in our present cultural setting. We'll now delve into the notion of the work ethic. Its roots are in calling, in meaning and purpose as related to work. We will see that—since at least 500 years ago—meaning in work has been connected to the idea of calling. We'll also see that that the notion of calling—particularly a religiously sourced one—has new relevance today.

MAX WEBER: THE PROTESTANT ETHIC AND THE SPIRIT OF CAPITALISM

The argument that calling has been embedded in capitalism—or even that it is, as some argue, responsible for it—goes back well over a century. Influential German sociologist Max Weber (1864–1920) made perhaps the most powerful arguments in this connection. The historian R. H. Tawney, in his foreword to an edition of Weber's *The Protestant Ethic and the Spirit of Capitalism*, notes that

> the central idea to which Weber appeals in confirmation of his theory is expressed in the characteristic phrase "a calling" . . . To the Calvinist, Weber argues, the calling is not a condition in which the individual is born, but a strenuous and exacting enterprise to be chosen by himself, and to be pursued with a sense of religious responsibility. (ibid., 2)

Weber was the first to identify an idea that many had already had a sense of. Namely, that there is a connection between work and faith; and that work is infused with a spiritual purpose.

For Weber, the connection between the religious sense of calling and its affirmation through success in the marketplace is clear. *Spirit of Capitalism* notes that

> The earning of money within the modern economic order is, so long as it is done legally, the result and the expression of virtue and proficiency in a calling; and this virtue and proficiency are, as it is now not difficult to see, the real Alpha and Omega of [Benjamin] Franklin's ethic (ibid., 53–54).

Weber also notes that "The only way of living acceptably to God was not to surpass worldly morality in monastic asceticism, but solely through the fulfillment of the obligations imposed upon the individuals by his position in the world. That was his calling" (ibid., 80).

This new notion existed in opposition to other prominent worldviews of the time. For example, the Catholic notion held that some callings were "sacred" and of a higher nature—such as that of persons engaged in full-time ministerial work—while the majority of the flock was engaged in secular work to which there was no especial calling attached. But in contrast, this new Protestant notion said that a call could be available to all. The Protestant notion of calling finds its roots in Martin Luther. Weber explains that Luther emphasized that "the fulfillment of worldly duties is under all circumstances the only way to live acceptably to God. It and it alone is the will of God, and hence every legitimate calling has exactly the same worth in the sight of God" (ibid., 81).

Weber explains the consequences thusly: "The effect of the Reformation as such was only that, as compared with the Catholic attitude, the moral emphasis on and the religious sanction of, organized worldly labor in a calling was mightily increased" (ibid., 82).

The way in which the Protestant ethic developed after Luther's initial formulation varied, but it maintained its thrust as a game-changing idea. Luther had contributed to a new concept of vocation or "calling," which had a great impact on the practice of faith: all activities, from the profound to the mundane, could be done for the glory of God and as part of one's calling.

Weber also saw a connection between calling and the idea of asceticism. This original link is interesting because its original tie to asceticism has long since vanished. Weber explains that wealth is

> bad ethically only in so far as it is a temptation to idleness and sinful enjoyment of life, and its acquisition is bad only when it is with the purpose of later living merrily and without care. But as a performance of duty in a calling it is not only morally permissible, but actually enjoined (ibid., 163).

In short, as long as it does not lead to vice, wealth is a practical way of confirming one's salvation. Later in his book, Weber becomes a bit clearer about his thoughts on the connection between calling and wealth accumulation:

> For, in conformity with the Old Testament and in analogy to the ethical valuation of good works, asceticism looked upon the pursuit of wealth as an end in itself as highly reprehensible; but the attainment of it as a fruits of labor in a calling was a sign of God's blessing. And even more important: the religious valuation of restless, continuous, systematic work in a worldly calling, as the highest means to asceticism, and at the same time the surest and most evident proof of rebirth and genuine faith, must have been the most powerful conceivable lever for the expansion of that attitude towards life which we have here called *the spirit of capitalism* [emphasis added] (ibid., 172).

This is an excellent summary of the connections many people feel between calling, wealth accumulation, and asceticism—and also of the greater link to the collective societal notion evidenced in the spirit of capitalism.

Some historians often characterize the entire Western capitalist system as being fueled by (and essentially rooted in) the Protestant work ethic. For many, this is now accepted without question. However, in Western society, over time, asceticism dwindled, but calling lived on. We can now characterize what remains as the Judeo-Christian or Western approach to calling.

THE JUDEO-CHRISTIAN APPROACH TO CALLING

As we've just seen, the notion of calling has a history that goes back hundreds of years. In fact, it was part of the societal lexicon in Shakespeare's day. Francis Friar, in "Much Ado About Nothing," written in 1598–99, laments, "Trust not my reading nor my observations, Which with experimental seal doth warrant The tenor of my book; trust not my age, My reverence, calling, nor divinity . . ." From the 1500s to the present, there have been multiple definitions of calling. In the context of this chapter, we will provide a representative Protestant point of view.

The Protestant approach to calling began with Martin Luther, who emphasized the equality of all callings and the elimination of a distinction between the sacred and the secular. There are thus clear differences within contemporary Christianity. In most conceptions, there are two places whence a calling can derive—from God, or from within oneself.

In this part of the chapter, we will focus on outlining a normative approach to calling. This will help us to understand how its adherents approach the notion of calling, which still influences how society understands the concept of calling. The Judeo-Christian approach to calling is based on several factors.

- First, it is based on the theological framework: what biblical sources say about calling.
- Second, it is based on the practice of calling in the marketplace.

For Christians, an empowering ecclesiastical reality is that God calls them. For Christians, called people have meaning in their life and work. Christians hope to be called.

But distinguishing the Christian approach to calling from others—whether religious or otherwise—is not an easy task. As the theologian Michael Novak notes, "The secular language of self-knowledge, identity, self-fulfillment, and the pursuit of personal happiness has been so interblended with the traditional Jewish-Christian-Muslim sense of calling for thousands of years that it is not easy to pull them apart."

What does it mean to be called?

In contemporary society, the word "calling" is often replaced by the more common word "vocation." But for our purposes, they are the same thing.

The word "vocation" comes from the Latin *vocare*, which literally means calling. Unfortunately, the word "vocation" is now synonymous with "occupation." This creates confusion, because having an occupation is only part of what it means to be called. Why? Because the word "calling" implies a caller. Who is calling? It can be God, or it can be a force from within. But from a Christian perspective, for there to be a "callee" there must also be a caller.

Whether they come from within or without, callings have four distinctive components.

1. We are called to more than an occupation

In the Bible, a calling is a comprehensive summons by God—first to God himself, then to a way of life, and finally to service. This tradition is encapsulated in three words: **belonging** (so Paul says that God has called us "into fellowship with his Son, Jesus Christ our Lord," 1 Cor 1:9); **being** (several passages in the New Testament describe our calling into a way of life, for example, "You . . . were called to be free," Gal 5:13); and **doing** (here, we have multiple references to God's calling people "according to his purpose," Rom 8:28). So Christians are called to *someone* before they are called to do *something*. This calling is not just to a specific work, but also to a way of life. Namely, one that involves love, freedom, holiness, and hope. And everyone, without exception, can be called. For example, the Apostle Paul writes to the whole people, "As a prisoner for the Lord, then, I urge you to walk worthy of the calling you have received" (Eph 4:1). Later, the Bible states, "Each one should use whatever gift he has received to serve others, faithfully administering God's grace in its various forms" (1 Pet 4:10). The sociologist Os Guinness summarizes the experience of being called in these memorable words:

> Calling is the truth that God calls us to himself so decisively that everything we are, everything we do, and everything we have is invested with a special devotion, dynamism, and direction lived out as a response to his summons and service.

But which Christians are called?

2. All are called

The vast majority of Christian business people view themselves as called. In the predominant Christian view, one can be called to the clergy or to a selfless devotion, but one can also be called in the world of business. These are all callings, and one is not better than another. Under this worldview, human beings are called to develop the potential of creation, to embellish and improve human life, to build community on earth, to facilitate global enrichment and unity, to create wealth, to alleviate poverty, and to invest in heaven. Many of these Christian vestiges are alive today in the corporate world in very visible ways, in addition to other places.

3. We are equipped for our calling

Christians believe God calls us by equipping us to serve in specific ways. Although some people make a distinction between talents (natural abilities) and spiritual gifts (as outlined by the Apostle Paul), it's important for our purposes to keep in mind that wherever it comes from, a calling is a calling.

Many Christian businesspeople in particular sense God's call through their gifts. For example, nany entrepreneurial leaders identified their success as coming from people skills, personality strengths, and management skills. These elements are sometimes referred to as "social intelligence"—the so-called soft skills that are vital to success but that are rarely taught in business school. These can be natural, innate strengths that can seem to result from being called. Many, in fact, feel that these innate strengths drive them, and/or that they have little choice in the matter of where they are led by them. As Elizabeth O'Connor notes in her book, *Journey Inward-Journey Outward,*

> Our obedience and surrender to God are in large part our obedience and surrender to our gifts. This is the message wrapped up in the parable of the talents. Our gifts are on loan. We are responsible for spending them in the world, and we are held accountable.

4. What calling means

Stephen K. Green, former CEO and Chairman of HSBC, provides some good insight on the nature of calling. He recounted that as a student he was called to full-time clerical ministry. He then ended up spending 28 years as a banker and then three years as trade minister in the British government. He explained that

I believe that that was a calling. I think Christians should always expect to have a specific calling, meaning that they perceive that they are doing what they are called by God to do using the gifts that they have been given. That doesn't mean being in full time church ministry.

Green goes on to say that he views calling in two ways. Firstly, he says:

You have to be able to tell yourself that what you are doing is going to be making some form of a contribution to the common good, to social well-being. That goes for whatever you are doing, whether you are a clergy person, doctor, teacher or banker. For me, it was important that I be able to say to myself whilst in the financial services sector that I am doing what I am called to do, that I can see why I am being called to do that and that I can see how it is making a difference.

Then he also talks about the manifestation of calling in terms of a person's actions:

I think that there are obvious challenges for how you comport yourself in terms of ethical codes. How do you handle issues, all the way from the obvious to the subtle but profoundly important? How do you manage expenses? How do you deal with other people? Do you lie to other people? Are you being honest with people for whom you are responsible about how they are doing at work? Are you being honest with clients? Are you, in general, being challenged in the spirit by such questions each day? That is part of what it means to say that you have a calling. That should be true for bankers as much as it is true for people who are in what are sometimes called "the caring professions" (which are a phrase that I rather object to because it implies that other kinds of professions are typically uncaring. I don't accept that).

Considering calling from these perspectives, it next makes sense to ask about the value of calling. That is to say, how and why is it valuable to us? How would our lives be different if we did not feel called?

Calling helps us to "finish well" concerning three of life's major challenges:

1. Calling is the spur that keeps us journeying purposefully to the very end of our lives—we may retire from our jobs, but not from our individual callings.
2. Calling helps us from confusing the termination of our occupation with the termination of our vocation—the two are not the same.
3. Calling encourages us to leave the entire outcome of our lives to a higher cause. While we can determine many things about how our lives end up, there will always be mystery and things that are beyond our control.

Calling is rooted in the metanarrative of the Christian faith, and also subsumed by it. They are sort of inextricable. Religion and calling are connected, but also one and the same thing.

JOHN MAXWELL: CHRISTIAN-GROUNDED CALLING

Is the Christian-grounded concept of calling still relevant today?

John C. Maxwell, one of the world's most popular leadership writers and communicators, is a leading thinker who tries to answer this question. Maxwell has significant influence on leadership thinking in the world today. One of us met him at the annual Entrepreneurial Leaders Conference in Toronto on November 16,

2016, where he was presented with the Entrepreneurial Leaders Award. Interacting with him, I was struck by how much his life and teaching reflect the notion of calling and the idea of purposeful (or what he refers to as "intentional") living. He is a pastor by background but now communicates largely to non-Christian or mainstream audiences. Generally, he tends to be discreet about his faith in his many leadership books. However, in his most recent work, *Intentional Living: Choosing a Life That Matters* (2015), he does something different. As he explains in the work itself: "My desire is that as you read and hear about me, you will make discoveries about yourself, your calling to make a difference, and about your ability to live a life of significance, which you can start doing now."

He incorporates this phrase "your calling to make a difference" because it's something everyone can understand. Whatever your faith, you understand the idea of making a difference. This is important for business leaders to notice. Everyone can understand the concept of making a difference.

DIK AND DUFFY: CALLING IN THE MAINSTREAM

As societies have become less formally religious, certain associated phrases have fallen out of use and/or taken modified meanings. This is certainly true of the idea of calling. We have explained in previous sections the historical and religious origins of calling and how people approach the concept today. In light of the steady secularization of the Western world, the notion of calling is in the mainstream viewed in a nonreligious sense. The key point, for our purposes, is that calling remains a relevant concept for individuals and companies.

In their seminal work *Make Your Job A Calling*, vocational psychologists Bryan Dik and Ryan Duffy provide the following definition of "calling" as

a transcendent summons, experienced as originating beyond the self, to approach a particular life role in a manner oriented toward demonstrating or deriving a sense of purpose or meaningfulness and that holds other-oriented values and goals as primary sources of motivation.

They carefully incorporate the term "transcendent" but do not specifically refer to a divine source of guidance.

They see a link between a person's self-identity as a "called person" and that person's expectations around work. Elsewhere in the work, Dik and Duffy observe that "anywhere from one-third to [. . .] 68% [of people] indicate that the concept of calling is relevant to how they view their work." This is a significant statistic.

How many companies understand and accommodate something that is relevant to fully two-thirds of their employees? As we have reiterated, the companies that fail to recognize this aspect of their employees' lives do so to their own detriment. Further, the connection between calling and the impact it has on how employees view their work and function in the workplace is both obvious and startling.

Dik and Duffy further note that "People with callings are more confident that they can make good decisions about their careers, more committed to their jobs and organizations, more intrinsically motivated and engaged, and more satisfied with their jobs." This makes sense. Yet ask yourself: do companies truly act as though they were aware of this?

If you believed this, how would *you* change or update your business practices?

The logical consequences of this link between calling and perceptions around work are significant for corporations and related directly to questions of how to motivate, engage, and retain employees. Dik and Duffy explain that "The more closely your life goals and career goals align, the more likely you are to experience your work as meaningful, in support of your broader sense of purpose in life." This is precisely the thrust of this book, particularly applied in relation to how organizations interact with their employees, or what we call service leadership.

Dik and Duffy also point out that "approaching work as a calling seems a good strategy for cultivating a broader, global sense of meaning in life." This is a great idea. Employees may never have thought about their work in relation to a calling before. Callings typically concern the notion of service. By cultivating a workplace that facilitates employees pursuing a calling, a service culture and ultimately a culture of service leadership can evolve.

And people with a calling perform better! According to Dik and Duffy, "This pattern of results is consistent across many studies: having the motivation to help others can lead people to perform better, to work more productively, and to commit more deeply to their jobs."

Yet too few companies act on this fact—and consequently, they miss out on potential productivity and satisfaction in their workers.

Dik and Duffy note about "boomers" (born 1949–64) and "millennials" (1977–95): "the two largest generational cohorts in today's workforce (1) see financial gain as a secondary consideration in evaluating their place of employment, (2) place a premium on making a positive contribution to society, and (3) seem to enjoy working with each other." The "how" of engaging employees is discussed later in this book. But what about engaging the current generation (millennials) looking to find their way in the workplace? And where is the future heading?

A MILLENNIAL'S VIEW: MEANINGFUL WORK

Adam Poswolsky is an American millennial writer. Poswolsky generally writes in an engaging and colloquial style, and while sometimes short on in-depth analysis, his work accurately reflects the ethos and thrust of his generation.

Specifically, Poswolsky writes about how millennials are highly attuned meaning seekers who desperately search for meaning at work. This can lead to job transitions by workers who are not engaged. For example, Poswolsky cites alarming statistics: "Nearly one-quarter of millennials have switched their jobs in the past year, and . . . the average 25–34 year-old is leaving their job every three years." Why is there such discontent or "meaning disconnect"? Two generations ago, having a single job one's entire career might have been the ideal. The last generation had four to five jobs during the course of their careers. This trend has accelerated even more. As he notes:

> A recent Gallup report revealed that 21% of millennials have switched jobs within the past year (three times the number of non-millennials), and only 29% of millennials are engaged with their jobs, making them the least engaged generation in the workplace.

Poswolsky also notes that "If the majority of millennials will have at least 15–20 different jobs in their career, it's likely that the trend of people leaving their job for something better is only going to continue."

Poswolsky suggests businesses address this challenge by looking closely at how millennials understand and engage in work. He writes about the myths and truths regarding the pursuit of meaningful work, particularly with respect to millennials. Interestingly, he frames his perspective in the context of calling, even if he doesn't define the concept clearly. He uses calling as if it requires no further explanation or qualification—and as if it were commonly understood as a way in which people express themselves and find meaning. There is no hint that the term would have any religious—let alone divine—element.

Ultimately, Poswolsky uses calling as a vocational foundation, advising: "Instead of searching for your calling, seek alignment between your work and your purpose (what you want to do for the world)." He advises readers to consider four things when pondering the nature of their calling and the impact they wish to have upon the world:

- Their unique gifts
- The impact they would like to have on the world
- The particular supportive community they want to surround themselves with
- Financial viability given their desired quality of life.

In the same turn, Poswolsky cautions that

> Fitting these puzzle pieces together is certainly not easy, especially in a job market where the U.S. non-employment rate among twenty-five to thirty-four-year-olds (which includes the unemployed and those who have dropped out of the labor force) is over 25 percent. It takes time and patience. But it's not impossible either. Instead of spending days, months and years waiting for your calling to fall down from the sky, instead of wanting to find the one answer, focus on asking yourself the right questions.

Another of Poswolsky's observations which is very consistent with Christian theology is that: "All work can be meaningful . . . There is dignity and purpose in all work." This connects direction to the contemporary Christian notion that calling is flexible subjective. Elsewhere, Poswolsky strums the same cords:

> Remember: any job, however unfulfilling to you, might be incredibly meaningful to someone else. Don't worry about whether your job or company is more meaningful than someone else's—this is a fool's errand—instead, discover what's meaningful to you. Not what's meaningful to your friends on Facebook, your parents, or your boss, but what's meaningful to you.

In other words, for millennials it is about their calling, what they want to achieve. In short, this is an opportunity for service leadership. For millennials, achieving meaning in life will involve finding meaningful work. This is a tall order for a workplace and an organization to deliver, but the more that a company can do so, the more it will have the loyalty of its employees.

Poswolsky also opens the door not just to a calling, but to *callings*, plural.

He states,

> Let's accept the idea that very few people have only one purpose, one truth, or one calling. Our purpose actually changes throughout our lives as we try different jobs, travel to new places, meet new people, and grow older . . . We have to define meaning for ourselves and accept that our definition might change over time.

Poswolsky's approach may seem daring and even a bit scattershot. But it may be reflective of how millennials think, and they are entering the workforce with these expectations. They are meaning-seeking individuals who want some autonomy and want the organization to reflect their values. Only then will they deign to identify with it. This is a higher bar than what many employers are currently configured to provide.

Millennials, according to Poswolsky, have the goal to find "alignment" of work with purpose and balance priorities. Employers can help facilitate this with an emphasis on calling and the search for meaning in the workplace.

CONCLUSION

In this chapter, we've examined the origins of calling in Western and Christian thought up to the present-day millennial perspective of calling (or even callings) as a mainstream concept. We have discussed the power of the concept of calling, dating back to Weber's analysis, to propel people's actions and economic activities. We also viewed the original Christian concept of calling. Hopefully, in doing so we have now laid a sufficient foundation to begin looking at how individuals approach meaning in work.

CHAPTER 5

SENSEMAKING FOR INDIVIDUALS AT WORK

I n this chapter, we're going to look at the different ways people use the concept of calling and the pursuit of meaning in order to approach work. In the postmodern world, a great deal of confusion swirls around the words "vocation" and "job." When you add in the notion of "calling," well, it gets even worse! We need to provide a clearer understanding not just of terminology, but also of context.

Vocation differs from career or job. As Timothy Butler, a Harvard Business School psychologist, explains in his book *Shaping Your Career*, "A calling is something you have to listen for. You don't hear it once and then immediately recognize it. You have to attune yourself to the message." The nature of attunement is central to this point. Attuning the mind and heart to hear an external call is a matter both of discernment and of habituation. Yet what we have established thus far shows us that many workers today have already made this investment in themselves. They are ready to hear a call. Excited, even!

By their very nature, callings that lead to a vocational bent are inwardly-directed. However, the consequence of hearing a calling is a public output, inasmuch as one realizes a calling in a work setting.

Today, though many institutions still shun the ecclesiastical-sounding "calling," they are only too happy to use the word "career" to talk about a lifelong and satisfying employment trajectory. Schools, universities, and businesses all focus on and emphasize careers. Career fairs, career training, and changing careers are commonplace. Like calling, career also has a Latin origin; it means "a road for vehicles." We associate a career with following a road or path during the course of an occupation. However, spending a lifetime in the same field or with the same job title is not the same as following a calling.

Researchers Kira Schabram and Sally Maitlis, in their article "Negotiating the Challenges of a Calling: Emotion and Enacted Sensemaking in Animal Shelter Work," offer some findings that are relevant to this need for sensemaking in individuals. Although their research was based on animal shelter workers, their findings are applicable in a much broader context. An important and under-examined issue in the study of callings concerns the *challenges* people face in pursuing a sense of calling and how they negotiate those challenges. Drawing on narrative interviews with 50 animal shelter workers, the research team identified three different "calling paths" that evolve as employees respond to the challenges they encounter when pursuing a calling.

While all individuals worked with similar passion and purpose, and faced similar challenges, those on different paths interpreted those challenges differently, had different emotional responses to them, engaged in different kinds of enacted sensemaking, and developed different accounts of themselves and their guiding purpose, through which they interpreted subsequent challenges.

The result was the emergence of three divergent calling paths over time, culminating in different emotional, psychological, and behavioral outcomes. Based on these findings, Schabram and Maitlis developed a model of the recursive process that could be applied in a range of work situations through which individuals negotiate the challenges of a calling. They also suggest ways in which employee responses to workplace challenges reflect different paths.

A TYPOLOGY

Our own extensive research demonstrates that there are three basic approaches that individuals take toward meaning in relation to their work and their role within an organization. For ease of reference, we label these "types." The first approach, or "Type I," is what we call "**Meaning Apart from Work.**" In this approach, an individual looks for fulfillment and satisfaction from their work, but not any form of ultimate meaning. This is a compartmentalized approach in which meaning and work are completely separate. There are two boxes: one is labeled work; and the other, unattached, is possible and even varied sets of meaning.

Second, there is the approach of "**Meaning Fits within Work**" ("Type II"), in which the individual is prepared to have meaning defined largely in relation to his or her work and often by that work. The employee may not have any specific notion of how to define meaning; he or she may be searching for a purpose and is therefore malleable from a company perspective. These individuals do not have clearly defined principles in relation to the pursuit of meaning, therefore providing the company with an opportunity to help define that meaning.

The third approach, "Type III," is what we call "**Work Fits within Meaning**," in which employees have a clearly defined set of principles—a more deeply-held world view—on how they view meaning in relation to work. The company needs to be mindful of the parameters of the person's established sense of meaning and then work with it, as opposed to trying to change it or redirect it.

All three of these approaches are ultimately insufficient to engage employees fully. We will look at them individually (to understand what is missing from each approach). Then we will describe in detail how organizations can implement an approach based in Service Leadership, and why it works when others come up short.

ENTREPRENEURIAL CONTEXT

To understand these three approaches most clearly, it's best to consider them in a practical context. We'll do this by looking at approaches to work in the context of entrepreneurship generally and entrepreneurial organizations specifically.

Entrepreneurship is fertile ground for autonomy, mastery, and purpose. Entrepreneurs can structure their own existence in terms of hours, focus, priorities, and the like. Entrepreneurs are high-propensity purpose-maximizers. Entrepreneurs can lead both large and small organizations, and they lead in the area of service leadership.

We must first understand entrepreneurship before discussing how an individual can approach it. While there are many definitions of entrepreneurship, there are essentially five tenets that make up entrepreneurship: (1) the ability to gather the required resources to establish a new venture; (2) a focus on the systematic pursuit of innovation; (3) a sense of personal fulfillment in one's tasks; (4) a risk-reward analysis; and (5) the ability to develop key "success" habits.

A first tenet is that an entrepreneur is one who creates a venture and gathers the necessary resources to pursue the opportunity. In fact, the original definition of an "entrepreneur" as involved in "creative destruction" reflects this aspect of entrepreneurship. An entrepreneur without the ability to garner human and financial resources is like a pilot without a plane—there will not be any progress. The entrepreneur must be creative in marshaling required resources to launch a venture. At the outset of the process, this can be difficult, and many entrepreneurs begin by so-called "bootstrapping." This means that while they cannot attract much capital to a venture that appears highly speculative, they can reduce their own expenses (by forgoing salary or reducing their lifestyle costs). They can also obtain resources by generating profit from their company to fuel expansion. Most entrepreneurs need to develop the ability to raise money from other sources. Even a good company is limited in its growth if it relies on generating its own profits. In short, the skill to gather the resources to pursue an opportunity is one of the very tenets of entrepreneurship.

A second tenet of entrepreneurship is innovation: recognizing, seizing, and pursuing opportunities with practical application in the marketplace. Management guru Peter Drucker, in his classic Innovation and Entrepreneurship, talks of innovation as the sine qua non of entrepreneurship. Innovation is systematic process that requires discipline. Innovation always results in change. Entrepreneurs view change as a simple fact of life. It's not something to avoid, but rather a thing to engage with regularly. If the core of entrepreneurship is handling change and benefiting from that through innovation, then the entrepreneur's "success" comes from his or her being a knowledgeable innovator.

A third tenet of entrepreneurship is that the individual achieves a measure of personal fulfillment through creating the new venture. Due to the almost inevitable cycles of the entrepreneurial life, an individual must believe in the value of the entrepreneurial life, itself and its benefits, and derive great personal fulfillment from being "captain of one's own ship." (To be clear, however, this is not some form of higher or spiritual fulfillment, pursuit of meaning in life, or the quest for calling; rather, it is satisfaction with a job well done and that one has fully utilized one's skill sets.)

A fourth tenet is that an entrepreneur needs to be able to perform a thorough risk-reward analysis of a proposed business opportunity. This is especially true when it comes to finances. A person who does not understand the importance of cash flow will not remain an entrepreneur for long. An entrepreneur must have the discipline to conduct due diligence before committing resources to the undertaking. A comfortable level of risk will depend upon how much capital is being invested, the size and timing of the return, and the entrepreneur's personal life situation. No matter how careful the entrepreneur, there will always be some level of risk. This can never be negated—only analyzed, reduced, and managed. The upshot is that the risk *versus* reward dynamic is an ongoing component of any entrepreneurial undertaking.

The last tenet of entrepreneurship is the importance of developing personal habits typically associated with successful entrepreneurs. While certain innate traits may be helpful (e.g., a certain level of intelligence or mathematical ability), researchers now generally regard entrepreneurship as a collection of skill sets that one acquires and masters. According to one entrepreneurship educator, Jeffry A. Timmons, there are six dominant themes that have emerged from what successful entrepreneurs do and how they perform: commitment and determination; leadership; opportunity obsession; tolerance of risk, ambiguity, and uncertainty; creativity, self-reliance, and adaptability; and motivation to excel. This is noted in Timmons's book *New Venture Creation: Entrepreneurship for the 21st Century*.

The five tenets described above provide a framework for understanding entrepreneurs and the entrepreneurial process. But they can also transfer generally to any enterprise. We'll now examine how individuals make sense of work, and pursue meaning, in the context of entrepreneurship as enterprise. We'll do this by describing three "types" of approaches to meaning at work we have described above.

TYPE I APPROACH: MEANING APART FROM WORK

In the context of the Type I Approach, there is no desire to have meaning at work, but rather to have satisfaction derived from doing the job well, competently, and using one's talents fully. In this context, the approach is **Meaning Apart from Work**. This Type I Approach is one way in which individuals view entrepreneurship and their understanding of entrepreneurial organizations. Individuals opting for this approach engage in sensemaking through compartmentalization; they pursue jobs that match their skill sets and separately pursue meaning elsewhere. In other words, their work context has no aspect of a deeper or spiritual dimension. The basic steps of entrepreneurship are a mechanical process. A person looks for ideas, does due diligence, tries to analyze the best opportunities, gathers resources, and then decides to assume some amount of risk and begins implementing a plan of action. The Type I Approach neither addresses the issue of finding meaning in life nor claims to do so. The entrepreneurial process is "**meaning-neutral**." When it's encountered, an organization must know how to deal with this dynamic.

Engaged employees who take the Type I Approach will challenge organizations. Of course, entrepreneurship can flourish in all forms of organizations—but at the core is innovation and creativity. Generally, employees will look to contribute, but they will have parameters around their personal sphere. They will typically not be interested in extracurricular activities or social outings/dimensions. They are not looking for or expecting to access deeper meaning in life. When an organization attempts to infuse its organizational culture with concepts of deeper meaning, the organization's message will not resonate with these individuals or processes; in fact, there may be stubborn resistance.

TYPE II APPROACH: MEANING FITS WITHIN WORK

A second approach of individuals to finding meaning in their lives is to define it in the context of societal influences that their work experience predominately shapes. External influences shape the worldview for these individuals, and an organization's culture can powerfully shape their expectations and desires. Put more simply, the individual does not have a clear, preconceived notion of meaning but rather follows the external norms of society to lead him or her. These external norms can include a significant emphasis on deeper meaning or spirituality. We call this the Type II Approach (**Meaning Fits within Work**). These cases are typically seen in instances where employees have either no, or only loosely-held, convictions regarding the meaning of their lives. They allow their views and desires to be shaped by culture. And culture, of course, changes.

For the past few decades, we have lived in a "spiritual"—though not necessarily religious—age. The age has been shaped by factors like:

- Deinstitutionalization
- Secular humanism
- Postmodernism
- The New Age movement
- The human potential movement

Collectively, these have provided the frame of reference for many workers. A loosely defined and somewhat amorphous spirituality emerges.

The values of the spirituality underlying this Type II Approach have a practical impact in the workplace. An increasingly common upshot is that we see individuals using a quest for success at work as the vehicle through which they will satisfy a spiritual desire for meaning and purpose in life.

In *Visionary Business: Entrepreneur's Guide to Success* prominent New Age writer Marc Allen states, "Business, like the rest of life, has a mystical and spiritual side." Under this paradigm, the work environment becomes the context for deriving a sense of purpose. Workplace activities become suffused with additional significance. Spiritual significance. Work is no longer merely a set of tasks—as in the Type I Approach—but a set of steps up a stairway of significance to discovering their meaning in life. This is often described as a journey that infuses work with a deeper directional purpose.

The five core tenets of the Type II Approach are:

1. self-generated personal narrative
2. living according to man's laws
3. purpose and meaning through work
4. niche for self-development
5. power to achieve purpose comes from within one's self.

The first component of the core tenets of the Type II Approach is the emphasis on what we refer to as a "self-generated personal narrative." Each individual creates a belief system through a process of self-discovery, unfettered by external doctrine. This form of thinking may be attractive for a post-Christian or nonreligious culture because, as Colson and Pearcey say in *How Now Shall We Live?*, it "assuages the ego by pronouncing the individual divine, and it gives a gratifying sense of 'spirituality' without making any demands in terms of doctrinal commitment or ethical living." Thus, to the extent that there is a divine source of wisdom, or global life force, each person has direct access to that source of wisdom—there is no ecclesiastical or other intermediary necessary. The role of an organization is not to reinforce correct doctrine or channeling of devotion—as in a religious institution—but rather the group simply celebrates their common experience. The emphasis is on experience rather than any specific doctrine or set of beliefs.

The second aspect of the core beliefs of the Type II Approach is a mechanistic view of the universe: there is no room for a creator or external force that may have some bearing on the workings of the universe. This approach has been termed "naturalism"—"the belief that natural causes alone are sufficient to explain everything that exists" (Colson and Pearcey). Within the context of spirituality, this is often referred to as "universal laws." The universe is said to function based on a series of laws, just as there are physical laws of gravity governing the function of motion. One of the chief universal laws is that wealth can be accumulated by diligent perseverance, and that in many instances a supreme spiritual being will reward honest efforts to accumulate wealth. Or, as the sacred texts put it, "as you sow, so shall you reap." Under this interpretation, the accumulation of wealth is the chief means by which a supreme being shows its favor with the efforts of humans. But it should be noted that evil or immoral efforts to accumulate money will not be rewarded. Under the popular interpretation of this perspective, only moral work is rewarded.

The third core aspect of the Type II Approach is the notion of meaning found through work itself. The starting point for this approach is: "Who are you?" and "What do you want to accomplish?" It's important to ask these questions.

One bestselling author, Michael Gerber, in his book *The E-Myth*, puts it this way:

But before you can determine what your role [in your business] will be, you must ask yourself these questions: What do

I value most? What kind of life do I want? What do I want my life to look like? Who do I wish to be? Your Primary Aim is your answer to all these questions (p. 135).

The use of the term "primary aim" in this context is the same as discovering your meaning in life. Under this model, the person's business then becomes a platform to achieve the primary aim, or meaning in life. As Gerber states in the same work, "Your Strategic Objective is a very clear statement of what your business has to ultimately do for you to achieve your Primary Aim."

In the same vein, the Institute for Enterprise Education, a consulting firm whose byline is "Instilling the Spirit of Enterprise," states that the meaning of that "enterprise" is "Taking initiative to achieve a self-determined goal that is part of a future vision, in order to achieve one's meaning in life, while sharing achievement with others." Another consulting firm in a different field, Profound Harvest, also adopts the approach of finding meaning and purpose through business by offering keynote addresses and workshops concerning how to use business "as a path to greater personal satisfaction, a sense of purpose, life balance and meaningful contribution to family and community." They also explore work "as a sacred calling."

One bestselling work explores work, meaning, and purpose in even great detail. Richard Leider wrote *The Power of Purpose: Creating Meaning in Your Life and Work* based on his "deepened belief that we live in a spiritual world and that every individual in that world has been created in God's image with unique gifts and a purpose to use those gifts to contribute value to that world." What "god" we are not told; nor the form of that god or the role of that god. These are left for the individual to fill. We are, rather, again directed to a kind of self-discovery. Leider then expands on the concept thusly:

Purpose depends on our intuition. Intuition is that almost imperceptible voice that leads us to our purpose. Intuition is our sixth sense—the sense for the unknowable. It is independent of conscious reasoning. Sometimes we cannot explain how we know something; we just know it. To discover our purpose, we must trust our intuition. The key to acting on purpose is to bring together the needs of the world with our unique gifts in a vocation—a calling. Calling is our way of actively contributing to our world, however we define that world (p. 3).

Later, Leider makes the case that finding purpose in work is well-nigh vital:

Without purpose, we eventually lose our way. We live without the true joy in life and work. Until we make peace with our purpose, we will never discover fulfillment in our work or contentment with what we have. Purpose is a way of life—a discipline to be practiced day in and day out. It requires a steady commitment to face every new workday with the question, "Why do I get up in the morning?" The wisdom to ask and the courage to answer this simple question is the essence of working on purpose. Spirit touches and move our lives through the mystery of purpose. That is the starting point where I begin my work of helping people discover their calling. In a pluralistic society, not everyone would agree with my starting point. That's all right. My objective, however, is not to express a religious or denominational belief. I do not wish to use my work as the basis for excluding people who don't believe as I do. It is, instead, the very reason for my acceptance of the many differences among people. Because of my starting point—my calling, if you will—I believe that all people have a spiritual reason for being and that our world is incomplete until each one of us discovers it (Leider, p. 4).

Leider's philosophical basis is clearly spiritual and yet completely nonexclusive; it has just enough content to satisfy basic spiritual yearnings, but probably not enough overt religiosity to be politically incorrect in today's work environment.

He defines purpose as "the recognition of the presence of the sacred within us and the choice of work that is consistent with that presence" (p. 11). And further, "Purpose is the creative positive spirit of life moving through us, from the inside out" (pp. 25–26). Other authors echo this refrain.

For example, well-known social philosopher and management scholar Charles Handy echoes the theme that spirituality is deeply connected to work. He states that

> We're all looking for why we do the work we do. It was easy in the past—we were doing it because we needed the money to live. Now it's clear that money—for many people and institutions—is more symbolic than real . . . We're looking for something more.

Handy ties the search for meaning to an individual's livelihood— the core activity around which his or her daily activities are structured. For him, this search for meaning is also highly personalized and customized.

In short, Handy's approach is very complementary to the Type II Approach.

A fourth element of the core of the Type II Approach is the concept of individuals self-discovering their niche—in other words, something that they are particularly good at doing. Work takes up much of people's waking hours, and an even greater amount of intellectual and emotion energy, so it will always be a focus of the individual pursuit of vocation and potential. While your purpose may be helping people, your niche will be the mechanical or technical thing you are good at doing. People will spend a lot of time finding their niche: what they are good at and how they fit into a given company or organization.

There are different ways to discover your particular niche. One technique is to investigate the core categories that constitute the talents we each have. Another technique is to use the familiar theory of multiple intelligences: linguistic, logical, spatial, musical, kinesthetic, interpersonal, intrapersonal, and naturalistic.

The last core element of the Type II Approach is that the power to achieve purpose comes entirely from within one's self. This is paramount. The ability to achieve success, to realize dreams, and to fulfill ambition is within the capabilities of each individual. The task is then to achieve that path to self-fulfillment by mining those internal resources exhaustively. The positive message for each individual is that you have the power to achieve the success waiting within you—you merely have to extract it. This approach can be traced back to the famous psychologist Abraham Maslow and his equally famous Hierarchy of Needs. This theory holds that all human needs are hierarchical, and that the most basic needs (like survival and safety needs) needs to be satisfied before humans can think about satisfying "higher" needs (like obtaining esteem). At the top of the hierarchy is "self-actualization." Maslow believed this was the urge to find self-fulfillment and to realize one's potential. However, it is important to note that Maslow said nothing about the help of any divine source or guidance in reaching this uppermost part of the pyramid.

A more modern author, Jack Canfield, referenced earlier, adopts the same approach in business but uses slightly different terminology. He refers to the highest level of being as the "State of Self-Reliance" which he believes has the following characteristics: "High self-esteem and inner validation. Motivates from within. Follows 'Inner Voice.' Is free from all needs and gives selfless service to others. Experiences no resistance." Further according to Jack Canfield, this level of being (this state of self-reliance) is part of what he calls the "Self-Realization Stage." In this stage, he explains:

You are fully conscious and awake, which requires you to demonstrate total integrity in everything you do. This is not easy. Very few people live their lives in this rarefied atmosphere. As you become more aware, you become less attached to events and the need for so many material things. Service to others becomes more important and you experience no resistance.

The Type II Approach (Meaning Fits within Work) presents both opportunities and challenges for organizations. In theory, businesses should welcome this approach if they can utilize it and maximize its benefits. The opportunity it presents is that individuals will be open-minded, without deeply held principles, and interested in experiencing and making sense of the journey. They will therefore be open to their workplace as a possible place of ultimate meaning. They are likely to be okay with being swept up in the defined organizational culture.

The challenge for organizations is connected to these traits, too. For such individuals may be so eclectic that, while their organizational culture may provide some aspects of meaning, it may remain ultimately unsatisfying, leaving the individual with an ongoing urge to keep seeking for more, as if in a state of perpetual sensemaking discontent.

TYPE III APPROACH: WORK FITS WITHIN MEANING

A third approach presents different challenges and opportunities still.

In contrast to the Type I (Meaning Apart from Work) and Type II (Meaning Fits within Work) approaches, we now propose a third option, which we call the Type III Approach (Work Fits within Meaning). As alluded to earlier in this chapter, we'll use this term to describe an approach by individuals that is rooted in a particular worldview and set of ethical norms that are the lens through which the world is viewed and an intellectual framework for assessing all opportunities. The challenge for an organization is that the more firmly these norms are held, the more potential disagreement there can be with a company's approach. The opportunity is that these norms may exceed the expectations of the company in terms of ethical behavior. For example, an employee comes preequipped with a meticulously high degree of honesty. There are also challenges and opportunities in how a Type III Approach relates to an individual's own pursuit of meaning in life.

For the purposes of this chapter, and to illustrate the Type III Approach, we will draw on a Judeo-Christian perspective on meaning, calling, and sensemaking within an organizational context. More specifically, our description of the Type III Approach will reflect a broadly theological perspective. At the same, time, to be clear, the objective for this book is to advocate for an appreciation of sense-making generally and not to advocate any particular faith tradition.

The Type III Approach consists of tenets that provide an intellectual framework—or what has been termed a worldview—from which to make sense of working within an organization. A worldview is the sum total of our beliefs about the world, which helps determines how we act and what we do. The Type III Approach overlaps with the syncretic Type II Approach in a few superficial ways. Don't get confused if you notice a couple of cursory similarities. For our purposes, the differences are more salient.

The first defining feature of the Type III Approach is that it's rooted in an overarching "God-narrative"[6] as opposed to the self-narrative of the Type II Approach. This narrative provides an infrastructure for the worldview. In the case of Christianity, it

---

6   This is often referred to as a "meta-narrative." We prefer to use the term "God-narrative" in order to contrast this concept more clearly with the "self-narrative" of the Type II.

involves the creation of the world and man, the life and resurrection of Christ, and the offer of salvation. In the context of our discussion we would say it is the precise source of "ultimate meaning." As part of this God-narrative, there is scripture by which to guide the actions of individuals, such as the Bible. In other faiths, it would be the Koran or the Torah.

These belief systems may also be exclusionary in nature. For example, one aspect of the God-narrative of Christianity is Jesus' claim: "I am the way and the truth and the life. No one comes to the Father except through me" (John 14:6). Of course, one can immediately see challenges to using such a precept to create an inclusive corporate culture!

The second element of the Type III Approach is a focus on living according to spiritual laws; in contrast, the Type II Approach is based on acting in accordance with man's laws. Higher laws are proclaimed within the Bible, the Koran, and the Torah. In the Old Testament, there are the oft-cited "Ten Commandments." These decrees from God are straightforward: you shall not have any other gods before me; you shall not make any idols; you shall not misuse the name of the Lord; you shall keep the Sabbath day holy; honor your father and your mother; you shall not murder; you shall not commit adultery; you shall not steal; you shall not give false testimony; and you shall not covet your neighbor's house (Exodus 20: 1–17). The Bible is replete with laws and guidelines for living. Jesus, of course, integrated his teaching with those of the Ten Commandments and clarified his dialectical approach: "Do not think that I have come to abolish the Law or the Prophets; I have not come to abolish them but to fulfill them" (Matthew 5: 17). Jesus also addressed the Ten Commandments (and other relevant issues) in the Sermon on the Mount, in which he provided guidance on a range of matters: murder, adultery, divorce, oaths, an eye for an eye, love for enemies, giving to the needy, prayer, fasting, judging others, and the like. When Christ was asked what is the greatest commandment, he stated that it is to love the lord your

God with all your heart and might and self. And he then stated that the second greatest commandment was to love your neighbor as your self (Mark 12: 28–34). Even this brief reference to some of the "laws" of Christianity reveals an approach that addresses all the aspects of the reality of life. These various commandments stand in particular contrast to the vague proclamations of the Type II Approach.

A third tenet of the Type III Approach relates to the notion of calling and meaning in life. Some attention to detail is required to distinguish the Type II and Type III approaches as concerns their particular understanding of calling. The basic distinction can be summarized as follows: the Type II Approach deals with calling primarily in terms of finding meaning in life through work, whereas the Type III Approach adopts a more comprehensive and holistic approach, interpreting the significance of work within the context of all of the aspects of life.

A fourth tenet of the Type III Approach is the notion of gifts (which can be contrasted with the Type II emphasis on unique abilities). Again, while superficially the two might have similarities, the Type III Approach is actually significantly different. Religious gifts are viewed in a communal sense and utilized in conjunction with the gifts of other believers within, for instance, the body of Christ. The discovery of gifts is not for self-fulfillment, but rather advancement of the Kingdom of God. Perhaps the best starting point for this discussion is the oft-quoted 1 Corinthians chapter focusing on the gifts as given to believers: "There are different kinds of gifts, but the same spirit. There are different kinds of service, but the same Lord" (1 Corr. 12: 4–5). Later in the same chapter, one finds a description of how believers are united: "The body is a unit, though it is made up of many parts; and though all its parts are many, they form one body" (1 Cor. 12: 12). This is a description of gifts and the interrelated nature of the process; this is not individualized self-discovery, but group discernment. A believer's mission is based on God's agenda. In short, rather than the various parts of the body—its individual members—seeking maximum individual (self) fulfillment, they are to seek fulfillment through a larger group effort. (In contrast, the Type II Approach treats the search for one's unique abilities as a means of atomistic personal fulfillment unconnected with a community of individuals.)

The fifth tenet of the Type III Approach is that the power to achieve one's calling is through "divine help" rather than "self help." A most basic doctrinal tenet of faith traditions is that faith is focused on God, and, in Christianity, specifically through Jesus Christ, his life, death, and resurrection. Vinoth Ramachandra states that a biblical faith is "the radical abandonment of our whole being in grateful trust and love to that God disclosed in the life, death, resurrection of Jesus Christ" (41–42). A Christian's focus is not on personal or horizontal strength, but rather on strength that comes through God. As Philippians 4:3 puts it, "I can do everything through him who gives me strength."

Norman Vincent Peale, a former pastor at Marble Collegiate Church in New York and author of *The Power of Positive Thinking*, in some ways gave birth to trends that have evolved into the human potential movement. Yet his focus was always on God as the source of strength, and he advocated the use of positive thinking to tap into that source. The bookends of *The Power of Positive Thinking* are Chapter 1, "Believe in yourself," and Chapter 17, "How to draw upon that higher power." In the preface to the 40th edition, written in 1992, Peale states that the book "is an effort to share my spiritual experience" (p. 11). He adds that "In formulating this simple philosophy of life I have found my own answers in the teachings of Jesus Christ. I have merely tried to describe those truths in the language and thought forms understandable to present day people" (Peale, p. 11). He further states that the book "teaches positive thinking, not as a means to fame, riches or power, but as a practical application of faith to overcome defeat and accomplish worthwhile creative values in life."

CONCLUSION

When employees come to a company, they will be at different points along the spectrum of how they have thought about the meaning of life in relation to their work. They generally have three different lenses and sets of expectations. Do companies realize this? If so, how do they deal with it? A fundamental aspect of service leadership is an ability to engage employees fully, regardless of where they are on the meaning spectrum.

The key is to balance the attractions of all three approaches. The Type I Approach may be, at best, ambivalent, but there are ways to have these employees fully engaged. The Type II Approach is perhaps the most malleable—these employees are generally content to have work shape their meaning for existence. And the Type III Approach may be the most challenging, as people with a preset view of meaning will be resistant to a different approach. The key is to ensure their view serves all the employees and stakeholders within an organization.

True service leadership entails the ability of a company to provide a vehicle for all employees, regardless of approach, to find meaning and purpose, which is a dynamic challenge. But companies that can do it will find boundless, surprising, and difference-making results.

CHAPTER 6

SENSEMAKING FOR ORGANIZATIONS

Mitroff and Denton: the spirituality context

Receptivity in Organizations

The previous chapter focused on sensemaking for individuals and how employees approach meaning at work. In this chapter, we will discuss how companies engage with employees who have meaning frameworks established through religion and spirituality. We will examine how companies take different approaches to their vision and mission, and to developing their corporate culture, and how this impacts the meaning framework of employees.

First off, we don't have to tell you that employee engagement is a hot topic these days. You can't read a business journal or a popular treatment on the firm without encountering it in one form or another. Yet as is so often the case with buzzwords, few really stop to ask precisely what it means. What does "employee engagement" actually reference? Can it be managed? What are its consequences for organizations? How does it relate to individuals as employees, as team members, and as people? How does it relate to other management concepts? Can that relationship be measured?

As it turns out, there are more questions than answers.

The conceptualization of employee engagement dates back some decades, but there does not appear to be any agreed-upon source. Nor is there an agreed way to operationalize it, let alone how to best measure it. In other words, the term is used loosely, and there is vast ambiguity about what exactly it means.

The lack of long-term research on the topic and predictors of engagement, interventions, training, or effective communication make it difficult to isolate precisely which employees can be more engaged. A strong academic link has been established between the way people are treated and managed and their attitudes and overall performance. In other words, engaged employees tend to significantly outperform their disengaged peers. Disengagement numbers may vary but run as high as half of the entire workforce, and, in some industries or settings, it's 80 percent of all employees!

Kahn's early definition of employee engagement was "the harnessing of organization members' selves to their work roles; in engagement, people employ and express themselves physically, cognitively, and emotionally during their performances." This definition has been refined somewhat over the years but still entails core notions of physical energies to accomplish their role, as well as a psychological presence when occupying and performing it within an organization.

In quantitative accounts of engagement (see, for example, May et al.), it was found that meaningfulness, safety, and availability were significantly aligned with engagement. In research spanning decades, meaningfulness has been found to have the strongest relation to employee outcomes when it comes to discussion of levels of engagement. We find a similar picture when examining academic and existential literature on "burnout."

The general agreement is that engagement is achieved in places where there is a shared sense of both dignity and purpose. This allows for a strong connection at the personal level and raises aspirations with positive consequences. In various Gallup Organization surveys, strong links have been established between engagement and customer loyalty, business growth, and profitability, as in earnings per share (EPS). Employee engagement is that important, and it behooves us—and any employer or economy—to try to better understand its options and the levers needed to engage with employees. The payoffs are great at the personal, organizational, and societal level.

MITROFF AND DENTON: THE SPIRITUALITY CONTEXT

Ian Mitroff and Elizabeth Denton, organizational change consultants, in *A Spiritual Audit of Corporate America* (2008) conducted one of the few, but very relevant, studies of religion and spirituality in the workplace. They treat the study of spirituality as belonging to the realm of "organizational science" and provide an excellent overview of the dynamic of spirituality within the organizational context. One way to view the findings of their book is to treat it as a way to understand how individuals pursue ultimate meaning within organizations. The authors identify one of the core aspects of spirituality as focused on an individual's pursuit of ultimate meaning (something we discussed in Chapter 2). And they make the basic point that while there is a fundamental difference between spirituality and religion, both are focused on the pursuit of meaning in life.

Their findings indicate that, as they put it, "spirituality is the basic desire to find ultimate meaning and purpose in one's life and to live an integrated life." This is an important element in relation to how employers approach being a service leadership organization and dealing appropriately with employees. Further, they find that "people do not want to compartmentalize or fragment their lives." That is to say, people want to have their spiritual sides acknowledged wherever they go. Employees are whole persons who come to work as meaning-seeking individuals. But employers, as noted earlier, tend to view employees as compartmentalized individuals who can disengage their meaning-seeking framework while they are at work. As Henry Ford supposedly quipped something to the effect of, "Why do I get the whole person at work, when all I want is a pair of hands?"

Mitroff and Denton also consider the difference between religion and spirituality. People are often reticent about being "religious," with its connotations of dogma, doctrine, and restrictions; this is far different than "spiritual," which is open, eclectic, subjective, and nonjudgmental. Mitroff and Denton point out that their "respondents generally differentiated strongly between religion and spirituality." They thusly explain the distinction:

> Religion was largely viewed as formal and organized. It was also viewed as dogmatic, intolerant, and dividing people more than bringing them together. In contrast, spirituality was largely viewed as informal and personal, that is, pertaining mainly to individuals. It was also viewed as universal, nondenominational, broadly inclusive, and tolerant, and as

the basic feeling of being connected with one's complete self, others and the entire universe (Mitroff and Denton, 2008, p. xvi).

People have an interest in integrating their whole beings in the workplace. According to Mitroff and Denton, "people are hungry for models of practicing spirituality in the workplace without offending their coworkers or causing acrimony" (2008, p. xvi). We identified this issue earlier: how do we accommodate spirituality and people's interest in sensemaking without causing discord? Service leadership, as discussed in Chapters 7 and 8, addresses this issue. But Mitroff and Denton pinpoint one of the tough challenges: "lacking positive role models of how to practice spirituality in the workplace, many people—not all—are terribly afraid even to use the words spirituality and soul." This is, again, an area where companies can take leadership, to establish clear and safe parameters for terms that can be used. Companies often employ more neutral terms such as "values." This is why in both business and academia, people can talk about "values-based" rather than "spiritual" leadership.

Another discovery of Mitroff and Denton directly underscores the importance of service leadership. Specifically, they report "one of the most significant findings that emerged from our research is the existence of a relatively small number of models for practicing spirituality responsibly in the workplace." The situation has not changed appreciably since that was written in 2008.

The authors go on to analyze approaches to practicing spirituality in the marketplace and their relative shortcomings. Mitroff and Denton clearly state the challenge now before organizations: "We believe that the workplace is one of the most important settings in which people come together daily to accomplish what they cannot do on their own, that is, to realize their full potential as human beings." Businesses need to fully appreciate this fact. As pointed out earlier, companies benefit from tapping into this situation to help their employees reach their full potential, and translate that potential into performance.

Mitroff and Denton describe five "types" when it comes to how organizations approach spirituality and religion in the workplace. It's worth reviewing these one by one.

First, there is the "religion-based organization," which represents a complete takeover of a business organization by a particular deity or spiritual school of thought. For example, a US-based entity called Fellowship of Companies for Christ International reflects businesses with this approach.

Second, there is the "evolutionary organization," which begins its life with a strong identification or association with a particular religion and, over time, evolves to a more ecumenical position. An example would be the YMCA, which had obvious Christian roots as the Young Men's Christian Association, but which is now essentially a sports and community center.

Third, there is what they call the "recovering organization," which exists within an organization where a critical mass of key executives is involved in recovery from an addiction (e.g., Alcoholics Anonymous).

Fourth, there is the "socially responsible organization," which is guided by strong spiritual principles or values that apply directly to its business for the betterment of society as a whole (e.g., Ben & Jerry's).

Finally, there is the "values-based organization," which is guided by general philosophical principles or values but is not aligned with either religion or spirituality—indeed, it can sometimes reject them both, explicitly and in strong terms.

Mitroff and Denton offer some insightful comments on practical applications as regards these categories. Specifically, they suggest "Spirituality is best attained through gentleness and softness." Individuals are sensitive to having something they perceive as being sold to them—it's too intrusive. Mitroff and Denton note that "They [the organization's leaders] are not to cram spirituality down the throats of individuals or the organization as a whole."

They caution that "Because Western societies are extremely wary of false religions in disguise, and rightly so, the leaders of organizations are forewarned not to promote anything that smacks of religion."

We agree with this approach, but we suggest that it be combined with another aspect of the service leadership approach. The company should have an open platform in which no values that conflict with those of the individual should be promoted, whether religious or not—and particularly not those that impinge on the search for ultimate meaning.

RECEPTIVITY IN ORGANIZATIONS

The previous discussion provided context on how organizations approach spirituality and organized forms of purpose-seeking in their midst. Receptivity to the notion of service leadership will vary within organizations, depending on the following factors:

First, the degree of responsibility held by the individual within the organization will impact his or her ability to practice service leadership. The higher up the corporate ladder, and the more independence the person has, the more access the worker will have to job crafting. Top executives will therefore have the most autonomy and greater opportunity for mastery of skills. (The bottom line is that top executives are more likely to create significant change than low-level managers are.)

Second, the age cohort generally matters. We have covered previously the various cohorts and noted that different cohorts have different ways of approaching meaning—with wide variance from boomers to millennials. Millennials, as discussed, seem to have a great desire to achieve ultimate meaning through their work. Money is not their main purpose. Rather, it is purpose maximization.

The third factor involves employees' specific training and, hence, the structure of the organizations they have joined. Professionals such as accountants, professors, lawyers and engineers appear to have flexibility over their approach to work, and their organizations are run differently from other organizations. Professionals may have a lot of autonomy. Other workers may not.

The fourth and final factor is the type of industry. For example, the high-tech industry (in many cases) appears to accommodate flexible work schedules. Employees work from remote locations. These types of arrangements greatly facilitate the pursuit of meaning by individuals.

We will now examine how some companies approach giving employees a sense of purpose through their work, occasionally crossing the line into "meaning" in the process.

Habitat for Humanity

Habitat for Humanity is an international NGO committed to providing low-cost housing to needy individuals and families. Its mission is "to eliminate poverty housing and homelessness from the world and to make decent shelter a matter of conscience and action." This combination of conscience with action rests in a religious tradition with roots in the rural American South. That tradition, a type of socially conscious Baptist and Mennonite Christianity, both inspired the founders of Habitat and in many ways shaped the growth of Habitat into one of the most prominent nonprofits in recent memory.

The organization has a defined and focused social mission, and it uses spiritual values to inform its model of development. By using affiliates and thousands of committed volunteers, Habitat maintains a relational sense of service to others. Moreover, its spiritual values connect to its public reputation and capacity for brand building. Those values and definitions of "humility in service" have served the organization as it transformed itself and its management and extended and broadened its reach around the world.

Cofounder Millard Fuller, in a 1999 *Christianity Today* interview, said, "Habitat is a small organization with a big idea, and the idea is that everybody who gets sleepy now will have a place to sleep."

Fuller established Habitat for Humanity with his wife in Americus, Georgia, in 1976. Over the next eight years, it garnered greater financial support for its various work projects, and it spread throughout the rural South. By 1984, Habitat had the support of former president Jimmy Carter, an evangelical Protestant in the Baptist tradition with strong social views. Increased support from a wide variety of private donors, including large-scale companies interested in advancing the social vision of Habitat, proved instrumental in taking Habitat's services throughout the entire US and far beyond.

Habitat has now grown into one of the largest and most admired nonprofit organizations in the world. As an international entity, it has affiliates in over 100 countries and has built over 500,000 houses. An estimated two million people live in Habitat houses.

Habitat's model revolves around faith in God, human effort, community, and volunteerism. This culminates in a bond to what is termed "deep commitment."

"We may disagree on all sorts of things," Fuller once remarked, "but we can agree on the idea of building homes with God's people in need and in doing so using biblical economics." (This is sometimes referred to as the "theology of the hammer"—using volunteers from various backgrounds to construct housing using sweat equity in house construction.)

Service is at the core of what Habitat is and what it does. At its most basic level, this links spiritual values to work and deploys those most willing—volunteers—who are committed to the cause. It also has an ecumenical aspect, meaning that it points out that differences between groups—whether on matters of politics, theology, worldview, or race—should not keep them from collaborating for the common good.

Organizationally, these same values inform the nonprofit itself. It has local chapters, known as affiliates, which must align with key tenets of Habitat's mission—while yet maintaining a certain amount of autonomy in working with donors, volunteers, and homeowners.

The relationship revolves around a covenantal sense of voluntary behavior and notions of diverse, hard-working socially conscious members of a community coming together. There are no preset conditions for participation—*all* are welcome. The whole thrust at Habitat is around voluntary contribution or service to a mission, in this case: to defeat the plight of homelessness and housing insecurity.

Cummins

Cummins is a global leader in diesel engines and advanced manufacturing with over 40,000 workers worldwide. It earns over a billion dollars a year on net income exceeding $13.5 billion in revenues. In the Fortune 500, about a third of its business is in the United States, while it has a substantial presence in Europe and the emerging markets of China, Brazil, and India.

The company has, since its inception in 1919, carried out what is usually referred to as "corporate responsibility." The founders, as well as its most influential CEO—Irwin Miller—were all Methodists, and that spiritual capital is in its DNA, cultural mores, and especially in its emphasis on the social responsibilities that continue to this day.

Miller, who joined the family company in 1934 and was its chairman from 1951 to 1977, is generally thought to have imbued the business with a new spirit of forward-looking leadership. Concern for the development and talents of its workers, a commitment to advancing the communities in which the company did business, and a long-term view of business performance and decision making all came to typify Cummins's contribution not just to the bottom line, but to society in general.

Cummins's management values and philosophy continue to influence the hiring practices within the company. It has instilled a belief in the importance of developing the individual talents of employees, rather than creating an antagonistic attitude between management and labor. Yet it has long supported labor unions.

As a company, Cummins has always believed wholeheartedly in the high potential of the people who worked for it and looked to create the conditions for the individual skills and creativity of those employees to take precedence. A commitment to employee diversity has become an important part of the Cummins's culture and system of values.

As a Cummins CEO, Tim Solso said: "Diversity will, I believe, be the differentiation between successful companies and companies that are less successful." He went on to add:

> It all starts with a belief that you want to be able to hire people from anywhere in the world with all the backgrounds—that you don't have some invisible barrier that prevents you from hiring a certain type of person.

At Cummins, employees are encouraged to bring their whole selves to work and become more engaged in the mission and success of the company. Cummins has come to define an espoused commitment to the individual dignity and self-worth of every employee within Cummins and is keen to be known for a place where this is not compromised.

This notion of fair treatment actually has been found to have a long-term benefit to the organization. Over decades, Cummins has developed a distinct reputation as a good place to work, and also a good company to buy from. This service notion of leadership colors every rank and file in the company from the top down and the bottom up. A recent Executive Vice President for Corporate Responsibility, Jean Blackwell, calls it "a long-term inclusive environment."

The company's involvement with and commitment to corporate responsibility has evolved over the years, but it was there from the start. Cummins has established two foundations to support its corporate philanthropy efforts and maintains 150 community involvement teams in over thirty countries around the world. Its employees donate thousands of hours of time and effort to local projects of their choosing around the world. The company has recently set three global priorities: environment, education, and social justice.

Cummins is a unique company where leadership is focused on corporate responsibility. It is intent on doing what is right and not just following the letter of the law. It not only allows employee contribution but also expects it, since it asks that whole individuals—in all their diversity—come to the job every day. This gives them greater meaning at work and in their lives and, as importantly, fulfills the company purpose.

Danone

This French food-products multinational, based in Paris, is the leading diary products company in the world. It is also a large player in bottled water and baby foods. Originally a small yoghurt maker founded in 1919, the company merged with Gervais Cheese and BSN, transforming into one of Europe's leading food groups. Consciously brand aware, Danone has adopted a strategy of employing joint ventures.

Danone's management principles pay particular attention to the health of customers, to the environment, and to society as a whole. The CEO, Emmanuel Faber, listed seven core and spiritual values for the company:

- Humanism through sharing, responsibility, and respect for others
- The desire and capacity to take risks, to explore alternative paths, and to overcome failure
- The drive to convince and lead, to exceed expectations, and to achieve excellence
- The desire to be challenged, to grow, and to take a lead
- The capacity to be imaginative, to look to the future, and to be aware of others, rejecting preconceived ideas and models

- Vitality, flexibility, and adaptability
- A simple management style that favors informality over formality and realism over theory.

The leadership at Danone is based on trust. With a strong business culture, Danone recruits only people who share its values and frame of reference. With a strong employer image, based on sustainable development, problem solving, analytical skills, and resourcefulness, Danone has created both an image and a brand that is constantly tested. With over 80,000 employees, revenues in excess of fifteen billion euros, an operating income of 2.3 billion euros, and profits of over 1.5 billion euros, the company has established itself as a giant in its fields of competition and has witnessed strong growth in both the US and in emerging countries. Its socially responsible initiatives are noteworthy, as is its commitment to health. Starting a social business fund has also allowed the company to experiment and show leadership where few other large companies have in the past gone. Danone literally wants to solve the nutrition needs in the developing world. These are demonstrating both measured benefits to the company and to the eradication of poverty and malnutrition. The clear thrust of Danone's leadership model and service orientation has led it down this challenging but rewarding path.

Lululemon—The "Cult Brand"

One company that merits more attention with respect to spirituality within its organization is Lululemon Athletica Inc. The company wears its New-Age, yoga-inspired spirituality on its sleeve. Founder Chip Wilson built Lululemon—based in Vancouver, Canada— from the ground, up to the point where it now has over 350 stores worldwide and is generating US $1.8 billion in revenue. Lululemon is listed on both the Toronto Stock Exchange (TSX: LLL) and the NASDAQ market (LULU).

The company has a unique ethos and corporate culture. Lululemon has evolved to become one of about twenty North American "cult brands," along with others such as Apple, Nike, Harley-Davidson, and Ben & Jerry's. It does not just sell quality products; it promotes a vision and a lifestyle, and it expects its employees to be ambassadors. Lululemon provides an interesting case study of how a dominant and invasive corporate culture can impinge upon employees' own concepts of the pursuit of ultimate meaning.

Chip Wilson wants the company to "elevate the world from mediocrity to greatness" and promotes a manifesto that is a mixture of about thirty maxims to live by—including "friends are more important than money" and "what you do to the earth you do to yourself." The manner in which employees are trained to become engaged with corporate culture has garnered attention. One particularly contentious and noteworthy feature is that Lululemon sends it workers to three-day Landmark Forum training workshops after they have been with the company for a year. These sessions are not simply about workplace productivity, but deal with the person's life and making changes for the better, as per the Landmark approach.

The sessions focus on self-empowerment principles created by Werner Erhard and encourage attendees to call family members and friends to inform them of changes they are making in their lives and to apologize to them if necessary in order to make amends. The Landmark Forum, according to its website, is designed

> to bring about positive, permanent shifts in the quality of your life—in just three days. These shifts are the direct cause for a new and unique kind of freedom and power— the freedom to be at ease and the power to be effective in the areas that matter most to you: the quality of your relationships, the confidence with which you live your life, your

personal productivity, your experience of the difference you make, your enjoyment of life.[7]

The Landmark Forum claims to have a "breakthrough technology." How does it work? The Landmark Forum

> offers a practical methodology for producing break-throughs—achievements that are extraordinary, outside of what's predictable. The Landmark Forum is grounded in a model of transformative learning—a way of learning that gives people an awareness of the basic structures in which they know, think, and act. From that awareness comes a fundamental shift that leaves people more fully in accord with their own possibilities and those of others. Participants find themselves able to think and act beyond existing views and limits—in their personal and professional lives, relationships, and wider communities of interest.

Employees are also encouraged to share their personal goals with coworkers. This goes too far, according to some former Lululemon employees: "I felt the lessons (at Landmark) were really valuable, but the format didn't work for me. It veered into the realm of being a little too preachy, almost evangelical" (Constantineau, 2013). This individual said employees were expected to have gotten something valuable from Landmark, and those who didn't could feel "a bit isolated" (ibid.).

Is the distinct culture of Lululemon religious or spiritual in nature? What is the line between corporate training and imposing a predetermined sense of meaning on employees? Lululemon is a proponent of the Landmark Forum. Landmark has continually denied being a religious organization—but it clearly advances a form of spirituality. As a scholarly study by Rene Lockwood notes,

---

7   Information on Landmark and its "Forum" and various programs is available on their website: http://www.landmarkworldwide.com.

Incorporating several Eastern spiritual practices, the highly emotional nature of the Landmark Forum's weekend training is such as to create Durkheimian notions of "religious effervescence," altering pre-existing belief systems and producing a sense of the sacred collective. Group-specific language contributes to this, while simultaneously surrounding Landmark Education in mystery and esotericism. The Forum is replete with stories of sacred miracles, healings and salvation apposite to a modern Western paradigm. Indeed, the sacred pervades the training, manifested in the form of the Self, capable of altering the very nature of the world and representing the "ultimate concern."

CHAPTER 7

SERVICE LEADERSHIP: ORGANIZATIONAL CONTEXT

Service Leadership Markers

1. *Clear Meaning Framework*

2. *Impact of Work*

3. *Work Is Not Life*

4. *Teamwork*

5. *Leadership*

In previous chapters, we've reviewed approaches to pursuing meaning and work and described how each of these had some advantages for leadership but fell short. Companies may practice various aspects of service leadership, but by articulating and defining the concept, they can deliberately and more comprehensively implement it. In this chapter, we'll use the following framework to analyze companies.

SERVICE LEADERSHIP MARKERS

"Service Leadership" can be characterized by the following general / corporate and specific / personal "markers." By "markers," we mean defining characteristics that reflect our concept of service leadership. The general / corporate markers make up the framework set by the company. The specific / personal markers relate to the particular role of the individual leaders.

1. Clear Meaning Framework
2. Impact of Work
3. Work Is Not Life
4. Teamwork
5. Leadership
6. Job Fit
7. Passion and Creative Expression
8. Facilitate Pursuit of Excellence
9. Personal Connection to the Whole
10. Autonomy
11. Serving
12. Listening and Respect

Let's review these one by one and learn more about their impact on service leadership.

1. CLEAR MEANING FRAMEWORK

The marker we will discuss first is what we call the "meaning framework." This is a cornerstone factor that all companies that want to pursue service leadership must practice. This is an exercise in good judgment and restraint by companies and their leaders, as they are not restricted in terms of what they do; they could in fact engage in "**meaning abuse**" with few repercussions, depending upon the options available to the employees.

Companies recognize the importance of providing meaning at work, but they also have a clear meaning framework: a clear delineation and recognition of the balance between corporate vision and mission and the personal dimensions of meaning. They exist in healthy interaction and equilibrium, with the company meaning framework not suffocating the individual's meaning framework.

In the last chapter, we touched on Lululemon. The yoga-wear maker steps over the line of meaning as it advances not only the importance of meaning at work, but also its particular approach to meaning at work. A company should not engage in practices that impinge on a meaning framework, such as life goal setting or weekend life empowerment seminars.

Daniel H. Pink, author of *Drive: The Surprising Truth About What Motives Us* (2009), was also referred to earlier. *Drive* is a generally insightful book about human motivations, including a discussion of purpose. Pink examines what motivates people and concludes that it is not what many organizations think it is. He explains that existing ways of motivating people don't work in many respects and that "we're intrinsically motivated purpose maximizers, not only extrinsically motivated profit maximizers" (Pink, 2009, 31). On the one hand, this is obvious. Most of us do some things not for money, such as volunteering in a nonprofit organization, giving items or money away, and helping a family in need. At the same time, people don't act as if it were obvious, as our economic system and company philosophies are based largely on monetary compensation. Pink comments that "economists are finally realizing that we're full-fledged human beings, no single-minded economic robots" (ibid.). As we have mentioned previously, the notion of approaching people as integrated beings is very important.

So, the company can be clear that it has a perspective on meaning at work, and where it believes meaning is derived from (such as a particular religious tradition), but it must ensure that this approach mean that it respects individuals' pursuit of meaning, regardless of the source, as opposed to being exclusionary by providing the sole framework for meaning among employees.

Martinrea

One leader who reflects a careful approach to a meaning framework is Rob Wildeboer of Martinrea International, in Canada's industrial heartland of Ontario. He is the Executive Chairman and cofounder of Martinrea International Inc. Martinrea makes metal parts for vehicles: engine cradles, cross members, and roofs. They are the second largest auto parts maker in North America in this space, with plants in Canada, the US, and Mexico. The company has grown from a small enterprise in Toronto that did no automotive business in 2001 to a worldwide company today with close to 15,000 employees, 44 plants in 8 countries on four continents, and close to $4 billion in revenues, with almost 80 percent of its revenues coming from outside Canada.

Rob provides a great summary of his view of work:

> Let me share the work that I have the privilege to do. In my life, my work has always been based on building things, or rather helping people build things with hopefully some positive influence from me. Work is a passion and a hobby. It is an extension of the human spirit. It is a calling (Wildeboer, 2015a).

Rob views work from his Christian perspective—it is more than just income, it is a calling. He also neatly ties in the fact that calling is rooted in passion. Rob further explains that work is a way in which we manifest ourselves, to the glory of our Creator and in the service of our fellow man or woman. It is about service. It is about the best in life. Work, in its proper context, is simply an extension of the best we have to give (Wildeboer, 2015a).

Martinrea is clear about its vision and mission. As Rob explains,

Our vision for the future is to be the best, preferred and most valued automotive parts supplier in the world in the products and services we provide our customers. This is what we intend to be. Where we want to get to. We believe in this vision passionately. Vision, without passion, is merely hallucination (Wildeboer, 2015a).

Rob explains the Martinrea mission as follows:

Our Mission, which is what we do to become who we intend to be, is fourfold. First, to deliver outstanding quality products and services to our customers. Second, to provide meaningful opportunity, job satisfaction and job security to our people through competitiveness and prudent growth. Third, we want to deliver superior long term investment returns to our stakeholders. Lastly, we are committed to positive contributions to our communities as good corporate citizens (Wildeboer, 2015a).

Rob clearly reflects a balanced and respectful approach. Although there would be an opportunity to advance his meaning framework to employees, instead he simply makes clear his position and that of the company with a view to encouraging employees. It is interesting that he frames his remarks with references to "calling," "meaningful," and "service." Despite Rob's strong Christian worldview, he gives no hint of an exclusionary perspective. In fact, much of the perspective provided by Rob, as reflected in the above excerpts, reflects many of the aspects of service leadership, as we shall see.

The key point is that although Rob is a Christian, he is careful not to impose his meaning framework on others. Instead, he seeks to live according to his Christian principles and hopes that he can instill positive values into the Martinrea corporate culture. Rob reflects an appreciation of and respect for the pursuit of meaning through a religious lens, which makes him see broadly rather than myopically.

Safe Software

Another business leader with a clear meaning framework is Dale Lutz, the cofounder of Safe Software, a business based in Vancouver, Canada, with sales worldwide. Safe Software makes a product that moves digital data generally, and digital maps specifically, from wherever they are in computer systems to wherever customers want them to be. Not only does it move data from A to B, but, along the way, it allows its users to rearrange it so that it becomes exactly what they need. Its customers include governments of all kinds, which need maps that they can adjust and share between different departments. Other customers include oil and gas companies and utility companies around the world. About 10 percent of its revenue is generated in Canada, 40 percent in the United States, and the remaining 50 percent is split between Europe and Australia. It is also starting to try to get into emerging markets in South America and Asia.

Safe Software has a software package that runs very quickly. Its product provides a fun and productive environment for its customers to work in. These features combine to make its customers very happy. They can solve problems that otherwise would take them weeks and months—Safe solves it in hours; these kinds of productivity gains are highly valued by their customers. They have a group of incredible world-leading experts on these issues because few others have bothered to assemble such a team. They are a leader in this area.

In terms of a clear meaning framework, Dale Lutz has taken the most appropriate approach. Faith shapes his world view. Lutz describes how his faith shapes his thinking:

> Because of my faith, I do not view my company's success as because of me. My success is because God has chosen to bless me, my partner and the people in my company. I think it would be very easy for a non-Christian entrepreneur to be very full of himself and herself. The Christian faith, for me, is a lot to do with keeping humble. I think that's one side of that.[8]

As Lutz explains, "I make no secret of my faith at work. At the same time, I'm not evangelizing on a daily basis either." In his mind, being a partner and cofounder of a company does not give him the right to evangelize to coerce hearers. Lutz explains the practical consequences, which may seem counterintuitive at first; for example, Safe has had a prayer group for many years, "which I intentionally don't go to." He further explains that "I have to be mindful of appearing to have a more special relationship with one group of people than others. I don't want that to be a problem. I want to encourage those that go to the prayer group. I also want to not discourage others that don't, or make them think that they're somehow lesser employees."

The bottom line is that with a clear meaning framework, he can be clear about his own beliefs and equally clear that he is not favoring any particular group. His hope, Lutz says, is that

> I can share my faith through my actions. At times of crisis some employees have come to me about something and

---

8   This quotation and all the others from Dale Lutz in this section are taken from a personal interview between Richard J. Goossen and Dale Lutz in Vancouver, BC.

during those times then I might be more open about my faith. I might be able to point out a spiritual side of an issue as something to talk about. So, in those scenarios I think it's fine. But in general I try to project a godly impression and hope that this is recognized and that people might be comfortable to maybe explore it with me or others or not. Nonetheless they know who I am and what I stand for.

Lutz reflects that aspect of a clear meaning framework. He is clear about the values that inform the company. Some of his positions may seem counterintuitive, such as being a Christian business leader but not supporting on-site Bible study. His approach reflects the importance of a clear meaning framework, but one that will serve all individuals in the company—whether Jew, Muslim, Christian, or of some other faith.

Stephen K. Green

For a reflective approach on the notion of a clear meaning framework, we will now return to the insights of Stephen Green, first met in Chapter 1. He joined The Hong Kong and Shanghai Banking Corporation (HSBC) in 1982. In 1998, he was appointed to the Board of HSBC Holdings plc, becoming Group Chief Executive in 2003 and Group Chairman in 2006. HSBC is one of the world's largest and most international banks. He retired from HSBC in December 2010. He was created a life peer in 2010 as Baron Green of Hurstpierpoint. He is Chairman of the Natural History Museum, Chairman of the International Advisory Council of the British Chambers of Commerce, and a member of the House of Lords European Union Select Committee. He chairs a charitable foundation, which mobilizes support for the work of the Archbishop of Canterbury in the Anglican Communion. Two of his books are *Serving God? Serving Mammon?* (1996) and *Good Value: Choosing a Better Life in Business* (2009). *The Wall Street Journal* endorsed

Good Value, saying, "Stephen Green is in a universe of one: the only chairman of a major international bank who is also an ordained minister of the Church of England."

In light of Lord Green's clear Christian convictions, how did he approach leadership while at HSBC? Despite his leadership role, he wielded his influence carefully. As he explains,

> My job at work is not to use it as a sort of pulpit to proclaim the gospel. I have never found that appropriate. In this day and age you may well find yourself, as I did at HSBC, in a company that employed 300,000 people, amongst people of all kinds of faith and none, and you have to respect that. You live in a microcosm of the whole world when you are at work.[9]

This is an accurate summary of the approach of service leadership: not to impose views, regardless of one's own faith, but to be respectful of differing views, with the intent of establishing clearly the boundaries of work and the pursuit of meaning. However, Green points out that, if a person does espouse a particular meaning framework, he or she should reflect that position: "Like any Christian, you must be prepared to give an account for yourself if asked, and you are personally and spiritually challenged to work out your calling in the way that you do your work." In other words, leaders need to be mindful of living out their calling and having that reflected in their work; their priority is not to focus on others and their shortcomings. Green also notes that a dose of humility in the entire exercise is useful: "You can't but be conscious that you don't get it right all of the time: the more you set high standards for yourself and others the more you become conscious of where you and the organization fall short."

---

9 This and all other Green quotes in this section are taken from an interview with Richard J. Goossen, via telephone, Feb 8, 2016.

You are there to stand for the right way of doing things. In dealing with people when it comes to, for example, performance appraisal, part of the job is to help people to learn more of the truth about themselves and develop in appropriate ways.

Green's perspective is that these different manifestations of acting

are all implied by what it means to have a Christian hope. (There will of course be many people with other faiths or humanist positions who say exactly the same things—and we should be pleased to recognize the common ground.)

Lord Green's approach, consistent with that of Wildeboer and Lutz, is one of respect for religiously based meaning frameworks. This is key.

2. IMPACT OF WORK

A second marker of service leadership is for the leader/owner to articulate the positive impact of the work that the company is doing. Employees want to be part of an organization doing something good. Izzo and Klein, in *Awakening the Corporate Soul*, cited earlier, note that "When our work energies are consciously directed towards a larger purpose . . . we find ourselves enlivened by a sense of soulful fulfillment." The company needs to continually reinforce the positive impact of its work, typically through its vision and mission. These statements usually articulate some emphasis on the greater good—the positive impact that is being achieved through the company's product or service. There are practical ways in which a company can communicate these messages. Regular departmental or company meetings, posting of vision and mission statements, embodiment by the leaders—all can be useful. We'll now look at some examples.

The bottom line is that the organization should be viewed as a giving organization—doing positive things—and that also provides a sense of giving among individuals. Individuals derive meaning from being part of an organization that is doing something positive that they believe in. The positive purposes need to be continually rearticulated and demonstrated in order to take root, and when the company leader is a passionate advocate, this is much stronger. Jessica Amortegui, in a *Fast Company* article (2014), cites a Stanford University research project that asked nearly 400 Americans whether they thought their lives were either happy or meaningful—or both. The two were not correlated. The dissonance, in part, was how the two groups approach social interactions. Happiness is associated with being a "taker," focusing on what one gets from others. Meaningfulness, in contrast, comes from being a "giver," suspending what one wants and desires for a fair amount of self-sacrifice (Amortegui 2014). As Amortegui concluded,

> In other words, to amp up the meaning in work, we must temper our taking tendencies and dial up our acts of giving. This is an appreciable shift, especially when the modus operandi in most workplaces is to continuously seek more time, resources, and attention from others. Meaning is premised on an entirely different way of interacting—that is, giving to others in service of the "greater good" (ibid.).

One important aspect of a company doing good is that this is communicated to employees with credibility and not spin. The positive purposes must not only be articulated, but they should also be demonstrated in practice.

The bottom line is that the leader should not only articulate the impact of their work—but also live it.

Costco Wholesale

One great example of connecting the work of employees to the greater whole is Costco. Richard Galanti, longtime Executive Vice President and Chief Financial Officer of Costco Wholesale Corporation, explains the Costco approach:

> I think that before CSR [corporate social responsibility] had a fancy name we were already doing a lot of those things. One example relates to how we treat our employees. Jim's [Sinegal, cofounder] approach came from his mentor, Sol Price, founder of the Price Club and president of Fed-Mart. The basic premise was let's start not with how little we can pay our hourly employees, and 90% of our employees are hourly, but what is a living wage? What is affordable high quality health-care? Let's then figure out how to make the model work with that.[10]

Costco is firmly committed to its low-cost operation, and that extends to doing good. Galanti explains,

> We don't seek publicity for what we do. Whether it's a local newspaper, a regional magazine, or even a national magazine that comes out with the most responsible companies in that area, we are often not on the list. It may be because we don't fill out the forms. We don't apply to the "beauty contest". In addition, once you start touting your own "accomplishments", you are not going to make everybody happy. There is always going to be some other more extreme view that you're not doing enough.

---

10 This and all other Galanti quotations in this section are taken from Richard J. Goossen, Interview with Richard Galanti, CFO, Costco Wholesale, Issaquah, WA, January 25, 2010.

The Costco approach, in keeping with its corporate values, is communicated to employees.

Galanti gave an example of the Costco approach to doing good: "We decided years ago that we would give away 1 percent of the prior year's pre-tax earnings, which is about $20 million a year now, on a $2 billion dollar pre-tax." About 30 percent of the total is allocated to the United Ways in communities where Costco operates or to comparable organizations in other countries. About 30 percent goes to seventy Children's Hospitals. About 30 percent goes to youth-related activities and education. Galanti elaborates:

> Every warehouse adopts an elementary school, and it can't be your kids' private school, it has to be a school in need. They do a third or fourth grade backpack program filled with supplies. They encourage employees to tutor one hour a week. Not only is it the right thing to do but it feels good and it engages employees.

Galanti explains the Costco corporate culture: "What Jim [Sinegal] doesn't want to have is a big twenty-person staff in community and development trying to spend half their time figuring out how to allocate money." Galanti cites an interesting tale:

> I remember anecdotally something very silly. We were collecting canned goods for something in the US. All of a sudden, we are having a contest to make the cutest pallet to collect the stuff in. Jim's view is that's nice and there is nothing necessarily bad about it. The fact is, first of all, we have a department that's bigger than it needs to be. Then they've got to fund their existence; they're coming up with ideas which take more time in the warehouse. We're a low cost operation and we can't do that.

As we can see, the focus on doing good is important—but it can still be consistent with the corporate culture of the organization.

The notion of doing positive things, and engaging employees, can take various forms. Galanti give an interesting example. He notes that "The last thing about corporate responsibility is sustainability. The nice thing about sustainability is that it rhymes with profitability in many cases." He gives the example of the traditional gallon jug of milk that has a square footprint and two-thirds of the way up angles up to the spout. This has been replaced by a taller jug with a smaller footprint that doesn't have a lot of extra empty space at the top of the jug. Just by doing that, and by increasing the number of gallons that fit on a pallet, Costco eliminated thousands of truckloads of transportation costs and eliminated hundreds of thousands of pallets being moved throughout the US and Canada. Another example is the water bottle: "There are water bottles that seem like they'd fall over if the cap's not on them; because they're so thin and you can crush them easily. Then there are others, like Gatorade, that are so thick you can't even crush them." The trend is toward using less resin in making the bottles. In 2009, on their private-label, standard half-liter of bottled water, they took out twelve grams of resin, which required their production department to put a few more "ribs" in the bottle to make it structurally stronger. It is still a thinner bottle, and just those twelve grams on that one item helped Costco eliminate seventeen million pounds of resin. Galanti notes that "it's environmentally responsible; so it's nice when you have that. Even though not everything that's socially responsible is profitable, we still do it. We recognize we can't be everything to everybody; we do what we think is right." The good news for Costco is that it's such a small amount per bottle; they're actually saving the customer money and making a little more money.

Galanti provides great insights into how a large company like Costco can do good things. Not only do they do traditional things like supporting a charity, but they can pay people well and push some positive sustainable initiative through to their suppliers.

Employees are far more likely to view their work as meaning when their employer is doing positive things.

ServiceMaster

Another great example of a company providing meaningful work by focusing on the big picture of the good work being done is ServiceMaster. C. William Pollard had a long career as the leader of ServiceMaster, which provides residential and commercial services, including cleaning and pest control. Bill, now in his eighties, has the bearing of a man of great wisdom who has lived his life with a clear sense of calling. Over a twenty-fve-year period, from 1977 to 2002, Bill participated in the leadership of the ServiceMaster Company and served not once but twice as its CEO. He also served as Chairman of the Board of ServiceMaster from 1990 to April 2002 and was elected Chairman Emeritus in 2002, when he retired from the Board. During his leadership of ServiceMaster, the company was recognized by *Fortune* magazine as the number one service company among the Fortune 500 and was included as one of its most admired companies. During this period, ServiceMaster also was identified as a "star of the future" by the *Wall Street Journal* and recognized by the *Financial Times* as one of the most respected companies in the world. The company also achieved market leadership in each of its markets and substantial growth in shareholder value.

He has had the privilege of having known three giants of our era. He was a good friend of Billy Graham and has served as legal counsel and board member to the Billy Graham Evangelistic Association. Peter Drucker, the management guru, mentored him when he was running Service Master. And one of the investors in ServiceMaster is the legendary Warren Buffett. The ServiceMaster objectives were simply stated: "To Honor God in All We Do; To Help People Develop; To Pursue Excellence; and To Grow Profitably" (Pollard, 2014, p. 95). The second and third objectives are important aspects of Service Leadership, as discussed in Chapter 8. As we stated in earlier chapters, organizations need to help facilitate the calling of employees; ServiceMaster's objective is to help people develop. In a similar vein, employees won't be leaving for another opportunity if they have the maximum opportunity to develop themselves in their present employment.

Bill was in a particularly unusual situation. Most of his 250,000 employees were in low-skill, low-prestige positions—cleaning up garbage, mopping up floors, and the like. How can that job be viewed as meaningful? By putting their jobs in the proper context, Bill could create meaning for employees. They weren't simply mopping a floor—they were contributing to the functions of organizations doing great things. The employees could take pride in serving, regardless of whether they received any recognition anywhere else. Bill noted that an employee will see work as personally rewarding and satisfying when there is confidence that the mission of the firm is in alignment with the individual's own growth and development (Pollard, 1996, p. 22). Bill's company did a great job of casting the vision of the important work of employees to turn something meaningless to meaningful.

As an aside, Amortegui (2014), at Fast Company, cited a study of hospital janitors who cleaned bed pans and mopped up vomit—perhaps the lowest-ranking job in a hospital—who saw themselves as part of a team whose goal was to heal people, which suggests that meaning isn't about the job; rather, it's about how you view your job. To paraphrase Marcus Aurelius, "Work itself is but what you deem of it."

Hobby Lobby Group

Another great example of an organization involved in impacting its community is Hobby Lobby Stores, Inc., and the Green family of Oklahoma City, OK, USA.[11] Depending upon one's religious views,

---

11 See www.hobbylobby.com.

Hobby Lobby may not be viewed as positively as in other circles—but the bottom line is that they are having a significant impact in their communities and the United States as a whole. How did all this start? With $600 in 1970, the Green family started Hobby Lobby Stores, Inc., in their living room. David Green turned Hobby Lobby into one of the most successful companies in its market niche in the U.S., with over 600 locations (all of which are closed on Sundays) and generating approximately $4 billion in revenue. *Forbes* ranks the Green family among US billionaires and has reported on the family's staggering generosity (Solomon, 2012). The Green Family has donated more than $700 million, primarily to various evangelical Christian causes and educational institutions. Mart Green told me that his family is committed to giving away 50 percent of the profits generated from its business.

What is the motivation of the Green Family? As stated on the corporate website, Hobby Lobby is committed to "Honoring the Lord in all we do by operating the company in a manner consistent with biblical principles" and "providing a return on the owner's investment, sharing the Lord's blessings with our employees, and investing in our community."[12] The website further states that "We believe that it is by God's grace and provision that Hobby Lobby has endured. He has been faithful in the past, and we trust Him for our future." David's son, Mart, is Chairman of the Board. He grew up in the family business. Mart told us that his father believes that every extra dollar they make is more financial resources for charitable causes. Mart explained that his father is simply stewarding his resources: the best use of his time is to keep doing more of the same: growing profitability and expanding capacity to give to worthwhile causes.

Likewise, Mart is also living out his calling by carefully stewarding his own opportunities to have an impact in society. The family business gives him untold opportunities for influence in a

---

12 See www.hobbylobby.com.

secular society. At 19, Mart established Mardel, with 35 Christian and educational supply stores in seven states.[13] In June 2002, Mart founded and was Producer/CEO behind the film *End of the Spear*, which was released to theaters in January 2006. In January 2008, Mart became Board Chair of the Board of Trustees at Oral Roberts University. .

In 2010, Mart started a journey to build a Digital Bible Library through an alliance called "Every Tribe Every Nation." Its goal is to centralize, digitize, standardize and finalize the Bible texts of the world. This will make it easier for audio, video, mobile, and print-on-demand ministries to get the Bible texts that they need.

Mart has talked about the development of Hobby Lobby and how the business has allowed his family to have a great impact (Green and Green, 2014).

The founder, David, still enjoys work and keeps coming to the office. The second generation is involved in the business and pursuing charitable initiatives. The third generation is involved, too. Tyler Green, Mart's son, is involved in directing charitable activities. Since 2009, Tyler has worked alongside his family at Hobby Lobby. His current role as the Ministries Coordinator empowers him to connect with a number of partnerships. He also works to pass on the value of generosity within the culture of the company and family. The Greens are an example of how a company has been involved in various means to make an impact, whether generated on their own or in conjunction with other organizations.

Mark Burnett, Hollywood TV Producer

Another example of someone who is focused on the positive aspect of his work is Mark Burnett, President, Television & Digital Group,

---

13 See www.mardel.com.

MGM, and Principal, Mark Burnett Productions.[14] What drives him? He says, "I want to do something significant with my life." Mark Burnett is one of the top TV producers in Hollywood. He has originated four shows, which were top in their category every weekday night: *Survivor, Shark Tank, Celebrity Apprentice,* and *The Voice.* In addition, against the odds, he bankrolled and produced *The Bible* miniseries, which was picked up by The History Channel when no major network would touch it. He then did a theatrical release of *The Son of God* movie.

How does someone get to that position in Hollywood? Typically, not the way Mark got there. He was born in working-class east London; his father worked at the Ford Motor Company. He joined the British army and became a paratrooper, seeing action in the Falklands War. After that stint, he came to America, arriving in Los Angeles with little in his pocket. The best he could do was to get a job as a nanny— a British paratrooper doting on a couple of kids for some rich guy in Beverly Hills. He had ambition, however, like many immigrants before him, to chase his dream in a new land. He began selling T-Shirts on Venice Beach and learned a few things along the way. He then bought some property and began accumulating some money. He got involved in an "eco-challenge," which tied in with his paratrooper background—he loves adventure. He grew up with a faith, but it was energized when he met and then married actress Roma Downey.

He is very clear through his company about the type of impact he wants to have on the world. He has a high level of expertise as a TV producer, and he is channeling that into faith-based projects that can have an impact worldwide. Who else would have the track record, connection, and resources to get a Bible miniseries produced? Even with his stature, he still couldn't get a major network to take on the series. As he told me, "you still need to prove yourself with

---

14 The content in this section is from the personal conversation of Richard J. Goossen with Mark Burnett in 2005.

every project."[15] He is passionate about getting the biblical message to the world through media. He talks about kids knowing all the other stories—but they are biblically illiterate. He is passionate about uniting Christians for great global impact. He decried that fact that Christians are the largest and most ineffective tribe in the world and he has noted that "the world will be won when we are one."[16]

He launched the Bible miniseries, which did far better than people expected. He did the Son of God movie. This was followed by *A.D.*, a miniseries based on the early years of Christianity. He has recently completed the Ben-Hur movie. All of these projects are driven by his passionate faith and inspire his team. It is very clear what the purpose of the undertaking is and the impact that it can have in the world. Mark Burnett's passion and enthusiasm for his good work are obvious. Despite a hectic schedule, during his visit to Vancouver, he was exceedingly gracious.

Whole Foods

Another example of a leader who has a clear idea of the big picture and who can motivate his team accordingly is John Mackey, cofounder and CEO of Whole Foods. John Mackey dropped out of college and opened an organic food-retailing store in 1978. Borrowing a small sum, he opened a vegetarian grocery in Austin, Texas. Mackey was on his way over the next decades to creating a juggernaut company that sold healthy food to make people's lives better while simultaneously providing a good living to all who worked there. He has stated that his vision was no more complicated than that. Over the course of his business career, Mackey became a staunch supporter of the broadest role for corporations in society. He said, " I believe that the enlightened corporation should try to create value for ALL

---

15 Personal Conversation with Rick Goossen, Vancouver, Canada, November 14, 2013.
16 Ibid., Vancouver.

its constituencies—to customers, employees, shareholders, suppliers and community members." In an interview, Mackey has said that he draws inspiration for his corporate practices from a personal belief in Buddhism. Although he founded Whole Foods, it draws no *explicit* connection between this spiritual inspiration and beliefs and the approach he takes as a CEO.

But it is apparent that a wider sense of service leadership has affected Mackay in his many roles. His philosophy contrasts sharply with a more traditional view of the role of business in society in which a public company existed for the sole purpose of creating economic value for its shareholders. While Mackey appreciated Milton Freidman's views, he thought that corporations were a possible force for good. By allowing self-interest and altruism to coexist, Mackey came to conclude that corporations, and expressly Whole Foods, actually create greater value for their shareholders when they operate on that basis. Mackey has termed the resulting corporate philosophy "Conscious Capitalism."

Mackay has been at the forefront of a movement in the US and around the world to forge linkages between new corporate models and the creation of long-term shareholder value. His model of leadership is visionary and sees service as its ultimate goal. His vision of a company with a "deeper purpose," as Mackay calls it, beyond making a profit while also creating value for a range of interdependent stakeholders is more and more about seizing the day. Profit and values are not mutually exclusive in this vision. Instead, they are seen as complementary. Mackey sees this approach to doing business as building trust with consumers in a way that will over time lead to higher profits.

Based on a strong set of core values that underpin the business, Mackey has shaped a form of service leadership around high quality, providing organic products, delighting and nourishing customers, supporting all team members, creating growth, serving local communities, practicing environmental stewardship, forging win-win partnerships with suppliers, and promoting health and healthy education. This kind of capitalism is the future he believes, and other companies have followed his lead. The attraction for the customer is self-apparent, and the company is now highly admired by its loyal and most devoted employees who don't want to work anywhere else.

Pinkabella Cupcakes

The story of Margo Engberg and Pinkabella Cupcakes of Seattle, WA, is a great example of a company showing how to make a positive impact on a large scale regardless of the product—in this case a cupcake. Margo spoke at the Entrepreneurial Leaders Conference (ELC) in Vancouver, Canada, on November 4, 2015, on the topic, "Changing The World One Cupcake At A Time: My Faith & Entrepreneurial Journey." Margo Engberg is founder and operator of a gourmet cupcake chain in greater Seattle, a mother of four, and a faith-driven difference maker. Her Pinkabella Cupcakes is just 3 years old and in that time has expanded to five stores and more than 40 employees. Besides being the exclusive provider of cakes for all American Girl Doll birthday parties in Seattle, Pinkabella creates thousands of logo-embossed cupcakes for Microsoft software launch parties and has linked with Amazon corporate in the largest cupcake deal it has ever negotiated. She is passionate about cupcakes.

All of her employees are part of the mission of making a difference. This is sometimes easier in a smaller company where employees have more interaction directly with the founder. Margo and her team are engaged in various initiatives. They supply 7,000 cupcakes at a time for an annual Food Lifeline fundraiser. When she attended the Entrepreneurial Leaders event in Vancouver, the hotel venue happened to have minicupcakes as part of the dessert buffet. She sampled them and said hers were much better, and she wanted to make sure that no one attending the event thought that her company had provided the cupcakes.

Margo shared her passion for making a difference at the ELC conference and emphasized her corporate mission: "Our goal is to change the world one cupcake at a time." Pinkabella will soon surpass 40,000 cupcakes donated to nonprofit organizations. That's about $120,000 worth of the confections, in addition to funds donated to a number of charities including Youth for Christ, where her "right arm," husband Doug, is director of development for Snohomish and King counties. One hundred percent of all tips received at Pinkabella stores goes to care for abandoned children helped through Children of the Nations International. The list of groups the company has supported with donations is up to eighty-four names.

Gloria Jean's Coffees, Australia

Another example of a leader and a company reflecting the idea of making a difference is Peter Irvine, cofounder, Gloria Jean's Coffee, Sydney, Australia. Peter Irvine was a keynote speaker at the Entrepreneurial Leaders Conference, Vancouver, October 17, 2014. He has had over forty years experience in business at a high-profile management level. Peter started his professional career as a junior at DDB Needham, Sydney, which became the second largest advertising agency in Sydney, and worked there for thirty-three years. In 1996, Peter branched out into franchising and in conjunction with his business partner established the Gloria Jean's Coffees franchise in Australia. Since they opened their first coffee house in November 1996, Gloria Jean's Coffees has grown to be the largest specialty coffee retailer and one of the fastest-growing franchise organizations in Australia. Today, there are over four hundred Gloria Jean's stores and kiosks across Australia and over eight hundred coffee houses in thirty-nine countries worldwide. In January 2005, Peter and his partner purchased the international Master Franchise brand and supply and roasting rights for all countries.

Peter Irvine described his most satisfying accomplishment with Gloria Jean's Coffee. He explained that it was the opportunity to take a brand and grow it internationally. It started in the US and was in fifteen countries but they were all struggling. They had one international guy and he wasn't allowed to fly! So when we came on the scene we were a big geographic country, but a very small population a long way from anything. We set about and succeeded. People started to approach us and now there are forty countries from various parts of the world.[17]

An important part of mobilizing his entire network was to make a clear link between the work they were doing and the good that they could be doing. Peter explained that

We were able to support ministries. For example, we were able to support two hundred people with Compassion in a village in Brazil. Our master franchisees all funded children and so at one stage there were 450 children being funded in a village in Brazil. That gets me excited. We were also able to fund $100,000 fresh water machinery in Third World countries. There are an enormous amount of projects that have been funded.[18]

Peter explained how he got employees at various locations on board with the various corporate projects. They appreciated the connection to these larger, positive projects.

TriMedx

As one of the most important suppliers to the largest Catholic health provider in the US, Ascension Health, TriMedx is a privately owned medical services company based in Indianapolis, Indiana, providing

---

17 Rick Goossen interview with Peter Irvine, June 3, 2014.
18 Rick Goossen interview with Peter Irvine, June 3, 2014.

technical support for health providers. The company's vision is founded on its strong core values, namely: service to the poor, integrity, wisdom, dedication, reverence, and creativity. The company wants to provide what it calls "compassionate care." The company's apparent success is in providing quality care and services that conform to the spiritual requirements of its Catholic faith tradition.

As a spiritual enterprise, TriMedx has extended into other concerns of the medical economy and even into the most dire public health situations where most fear to go. Its foundation illustrates the company approach to taking the Catholic notions of "serving the least" through the entire health care system. The company runs dozens of short-term health care missions to many poor countries around the world. In addition, it owns and runs a medical repair center that fixes or updates medical equipment for service in for-need hospitals and clinics in remote places far away from the American heartland.

Operating inside the larger Ascension system, TriMedx is part and parcel of Catholic social teaching, and it is the very core of its business and approach to medical ethics and the medical economy, which makes up 17 percent of the entire US GNP. Starting with its base of hospitals established by the Daughters of Charity of St Vincent de Paul, the Sisters of St. Joseph of Carondelet, and Congregation of St. Joseph, the company over decades acquired other hospital systems and health care providers. It now has operations in over five hundred locations, in twenty states and the District of Columbia.

What uniquely colors TriMedx is its view of life. Its definition of holistic health considers impacts on health care and [makes] provisions for those who need it most. There are services it won't supply due to the company's beliefs. But this is a big business that is not driven by profit, but rather by a defined mission of serving. Its moral compass and purposes are moored to the doctrine of the Church. As a social service, the company defines itself by its critical role in society.

Service leadership is implicit in everything it does, from its vision to its values to its execution. Greg Ranger, founder, former CEO, and current Board member of TriMedx, in interviews restated that the company is truly mission-driven and is defined by serving the least in society through what he called "compassionate care."

3. WORK IS NOT LIFE

A third aspect of service leadership from a corporate perspective is reinforcing the message that although work is important, it is not your life. This is, of course, not always that case. In a report on the work culture of Amazon (Kantor and Streitfield, 2015), one employee who worked on projects including Kindle and the Fire TV device reminisced that "The joke in the office was that when it came to work/life balance, work came first, life came second, and trying to find the balance came last" (Kantor and Streitfield, 2015). Many employees said the culture stoked their "willingness to erode work-like boundaries" and that the workloads at the new South Lake Union campus could be extreme: "marathon conference calls on Easter Sunday and Thanksgiving, criticism from bosses for spotty Internet access on vacation, and hours spent working at home most nights or weekends" (Kantor and Streitfield, 2015). This is an all-too-typical example of companies putting excessive demands on employees without regard for a life of meaningful balance.

An important aspect of service leadership is the understanding and acknowledgement that work is not life. In other words, a company recognizes that regardless of the importance of work, and doing a job well, and making money, there is indeed much more to life than just a job. Companies don't always act this way in terms of how they structure the working arrangements or their expectations. By making the job the sole point of the employee's existence, this will ultimately lead to a shallow sense of their own meaning in life. There are many telltale signs of work becoming the sole focus of the person's life. This can be inordinately long hours at the office, taking work home, thinking about work constantly, work crowding out leisure activities, or the person's identity being tied up in work.

What does a proper approach look like? The employee can work hard and effectively, but they have reasonable working hours that allow the time and energy for outside activities. The company acknowledges and recognizes the outside commitments of employees, from family, volunteer activities, and extended travel. The company accommodates paternity and maternity leaves as part of the cycle of life and works to accommodate those employees.

Facebook

Facebook has adopted a number of policies—in the war for talent—that serve employees' needs well in recognizing that work is not life. For example, Facebook is enhancing its parental leave policies. The company has upgraded its policies with death and illness in employees' families. These are "rare but increasingly sought-after offerings, especially as millennials, now the largest share of the workforce, begin caring for their aging Boomer parents" (Greenfield, 2017, p. D7). Facebook now "offers employees six weeks of paid time off to spend time with a family member who has a long-term illness" (Greenfield, 2017). Facebook also expanded its bereavement leave to 20 days from 10. Sheryl Sandberg, COO, Facebook, is well known as the author of *Lean In*. She writes that "People should be able both to work and be there for their families. No one should face this trade-off [ability to take time off for family contingencies]" (Sandberg quoted in Greenfield, 2017).

Law Firms / Professional Services Firms

There is a particular dynamic among large law firms that present a certain view of work. Young graduates are brought into these large, downtown firms with the expectation of working sixty-eighty hours per week. If you are not prepared to work those hours, that's fine, but step aside, because there are many others who will do so. Some working at Wall Street firms actually sleep at the office overnight.

I (Rick Goossen) remember vividly on one occasion being in New York and arranging to meet one of my friends for dinner. The dinner kept getting pushed back—until finally we met at 10:30 p.m. This friend of mine was at one of these firms. The idea is that the young up-and-comers have to go through a form of apprenticeship, a grinding, to see if they have the mettle to survive. But the pace doesn't slacken much as the young lawyer proceeds up the ranks. There continue to be inordinate demands on these professionals. One unique dynamic of the legal profession is that the focus is generally on billable time—so this puts pressure on being able to bill a certain number of hours per day, per month, per year, in order to justify your salary and to generate profits for the firm.

There is almost an intentional imbalance in the lives of these professionals—not just lawyers, but other professionals in that category. People can by motivated by money, prestige, and great work to do for clients, but these are distractions in the form of "meaningful activity" that do not comprise a solution to "ultimate meaning." Thus, after progressing in their careers for a certain number of years, they begin to ask, "What is my life about?" and "Is this what I want to be doing?" As a result, there are many cases of midcareer burnout, premature retirement, looking for something different to do, or quiet resignation that the golden handcuffs will keep them in the rut until retirement (they are making good money, and there are no other options to earn similar income doing something else).

One simple reflection of this dynamic is that law schools in Western countries admit an almost equal number of women and men into their ranks, but the number of partners in major firms is heavily weighted toward men. Because of the demands of the professional firm, there is an inordinate amount of pressure on a person who may be able to handle it with a supportive spouse. In our present environment, many male lawyers are more likely to have a female spouse to pick up the slack. Meanwhile the female lawyer is less likely to have a male partner to do the same. This issue is only relevant because of the imbalance in the approach to work.

For these firms, work is clearly life. There is little room for meaning apart from work. Work literally defines the professionals at the firm. They make many sacrifices for their work. They want to have it all, but the long-term proves that they can't. Many things that make life meaningful take time—such as family, volunteering. The proof is in the pudding. Many of the people who became absorbed in being a good partner of a major downtown firm are typically divorced (at least once), have children with various challenges, and are often not in good physical health.

So these firms, of which there are many, do not practice Service Leadership. They have set up an economic model that they believe only works on that basis, involving a certain number of hours to be billed, to support the overhead. This does not have to be the case.

Coachify

Another company that provides insights in the matter of work and life is a UK startup called Coachify. This is a wearables company founded by Nick Chatrath that has developed advanced algorithms to help people manage the stress of business life and to energize their attitudes and productivity in the workplace. It is part of the workplace revolution brought on by technology. Chatrath is a successful former McKinsey consultant who did a doctorate at Oxford in Oriental philosophy, specializing in Islamic law and culture.

With a definition of intelligence that spans emotional life, physical life, rationality, and the realm of the spiritual, Coachify is on to something. Using Fitbit and the Apple watch and similar devices, the company can literally monitor behavior and biostatistical measures to give feedback or customized coaching to any given individual or team.

The intersection of technology and values is at the heart of Coachify, and the vision comes from its founder and CEO, Nick Chatrath. The company embodies all that we have described in this book and takes it to the *next* level. It deploys technology in new and novel ways, feeding it back to increase productivity, and it is based on an integrative understanding of the human person—a combination of intelligences that are fused together into a whole.

The mission of Coachify, which is a for-profit company in the early stages of development, is all about service leadership. It seeks to make better leaders by putting them in touch with their total systems and the environments in which they work. Realizing that people are attempting to make sense of their surroundings, want better work-life balance, and seek to be more productive, Coachify structures through its use of devices, monitoring, and personalized coaching a way to cope with the travails and challenges of the modern workplace.

Coachify has a distinctive vision. Big data are transforming many organizations' performance, and personal data have the power to transform personal accountability and performance, too. But data alone are not enough—they need to be interpreted and turned into actions. That's where Coachify comes in. It uses a proprietary technology and data analytics platform to provide insight into individual performance, guidance, and a made-to-order goal-orientated plan. Coachify has developed a unique product combined with next-generation coaching techniques to reach deep into organizations developing talent and driving a performance-led culture. Early trials indicate individual productivity improvements of over 20 percent in a 3–6 month period (measured by input metrics and outcome measures).

The interaction with wearable devices and the Coachify personal dashboard drive different types of behavior as individuals embrace the technology to set higher personal goals, including heightened levels of awareness about lifestyle variables that affect performance; and a strong sense of excitement, competition, and empathy with others.

Coachify delivers what can be termed just-in-time coaching. It differs from legacy coaching methods in three main ways. First, the device is always on. Whereas traditional coaching is mostly constrained by working around scheduled meetings, with Coachify, the interventions are data-driven, increasing personal impact and the ability to get more value from each day. Second, it's next generation. The amount of data available is increasing rapidly as wearables become more sophisticated and commonplace in the workplace, and Coachify uses proprietary analytical capabilities to deliver the right information and the right insights to transform this into action. Third, it offers the complete picture. Although a qualitative approach to coaching can be transformational too, used alone it can mean that many influencing factors are missed (e.g., addiction fatigue, driven by "uncontrollable" impulses in the vicinity of a smartphone, energy and stress levels, as well as fitness and diet). Coachify helps to engineer a reverse state of being.

Coachify is inviting leaders in the personal productivity revolution to take part in a more meaningful service-based way to work. It works with organizations that are already investing in wearables and rolling out corporate wellness programs. It also works with forward-thinking organizations and board-level sponsors seeking to create a vision for the application of wearable technology with coaching. It has a number of leading companies and senior executives signed up because they want to be better leaders, they want to be more productive, and they want to tap into a holistic way of leading.

Coachify is passionate about helping people to change the world around them. In the same way, it is committed to changing the world for the better as a company, giving one-third of net profit to transformational projects. The founder uses his technology, strategy consulting, and spiritual training and background to build the next generation tools for service leadership while employing the same principles and values in the company he is creating and bringing to scale.

4. TEAMWORK

A fourth aspect of the meaning frame is the notion of teamwork. We have noted earlier in the book that teamwork, and enjoying the support and camaraderie of team members, is important, but it is in the category of meaningful activity and does not substitute for ultimate meaning. Teamwork is important because relationships are important. When people work in a company, they spend a lot of time with their coworkers and their bosses.

There arc various ways in which companies can facilitate great teamwork. These can include various activities such as team meetings and company functions. Even having regular birthday parties for office staff is a simple way to establish community. But again, in a situation when a company must be clear on the line of meeting, it may be going too far to try to establish teamwork by having weekend retreats and coworkers sharing rooms. Individuals have their personal space, and weekends are typically spent on personal activities—not with the company.

As Amortegui (2014) of *Fast Company* notes,

according to Elizabeth Dunn and Michael Norton, authors of *Happy Money*, if you awaken any well-being expert in middle of the night and ask them what matters most in life, you'll get the same response: relationships. Michael Steger, international meaning expert and creator of The Work and Meaning Inventory, agrees. He believes that relationships are the ocean in which we find meaning.

Gallup's findings that the most engaged workers report having a best friend at work have become a well-cited statistic for good reason. If you look at experiences of those who report higher meaning at work, it is not what people are doing—but rather who they are with. This is consistent with a set of findings on what distinguishes our best days: days whereby we feel enlivened and truly thriving. These days include at least six hours of social time. In fact, even three hours of social time reduces the chances of having a bad day by 10%. Meaning is made in moments, and what matters most is the people we create those moments with (Amortegui, 2014).

Safe Software

Dale Lutz, cofounder, Safe Software, offers insights into the process of building a team. He believes that "The key attributes are to find people with low ego, who get things done and are smart. If you can find people that embody those three things you can basically overcome almost any barrier."[19] Interestingly, the notion of low ego has come up regularly in our research over the years. As Lutz elaborates, "The ego issue is a challenging one because we've had some come through our office and when ego gets in the way of teamwork and other things then there can be big problems." This is a considerable challenge in the present work environment: when people are taught that they are free agents and have a personal brand, they view companies as a step to somewhere else and are interested in their own progression. Also, people are hired based on their résumé, their own credentials and abilities, so they are constantly interested in building their résumé—not the résumé of whatever team they have been on. Lutz explains that "We've tried pretty hard to craft a culture of teamwork. The company is about 90-some people now and really it's a pleasant place for everyone to work. One of our core assets is our company culture."

Lutz is building the team culture in various ways. Both he and his partner are very approachable, which helps set a positive tone. They work to have group events. Lutz notes that

the company events such as our Christmas party are very rewarding. At moments like that I feel happy about being

---

19 Richard J. Goossen Interview with Dale Lutz, Langley, BC, Canada, in person, June 17, 2011.

an entrepreneur. We are able to bring together staff and have a celebration together. I look around that room and I see all those people whose families are relying on the work that we do and the fact that I can play a role in giving all those people a really good place to work and to provide for them also is immensely rewarding. The bottom line is that team-work is an important part of creating meaning for people in the workplace.

Eversunny, PRC

There are sometimes very interesting nuances to be found in different parts of the world. In other countries, the structure of business may be fundamentally different from that in the Western world. One immediate difference is the role of the family business. In Asia, business is family and family is business, and there is much greater integration between the two. Of course, there are family businesses in the West, but not to the same extent. Another element is that the business structure takes root in the specific culture. Asia is influenced by Confucian values, whether implicitly or explicitly So, the nature of teamwork would be very different from that in a Western context. Eversunny is a recent company whose main lines of business include iron ore, steel, and scrap sourcing and manufacturing. Based in urban China, the company acts as an agent between enterprises and is a large exporter of goods.

Eversunny may be a newer company, but its values are quite ancient. Confucianism's philosophies evolve around the central concept of harmony, which extends into achieving ideals such as coherence, congruence, accord, and coordination within society, art, and all human endeavors. This includes business as an enterprise. Eversunny makes an attempt to model its business on the classical ideas of Confucian global leadership focused on "cultivating and extending virtues and duties according to one's personal station and function within society." There are three principles here that are applied to achieving the ideal of Confucian leadership: transformation, timeliness, and harmonization. Achieving holistic and long-term objectives harmoniously is paramount. One of the first things that you see in a Confucian company is the emphasis on obedience and hierarchy. But equally important is the tradition of lasting and trusting relationships. This emphasis at Eversunny on achieving trust explains the emphasis on saving face and informs the approach to negotiation, a slow process where relationships are built up in a growing relationship. Once mutual respect is established, a contract may result. This style of business is inspired and imbued with a spirit of self and a respect for others that help to lend meaning to work.

5. LEADERSHIP

A critical element to the practice of service leadership is contained in the "leadership" component. Without good leadership, the practice of service leadership will fail. In this section, we will review a number of examples of leadership. To be clear, we are not highlighting companies that practice "servant leadership," as defined previously. Instead, we are highlighting leaders and their ability to practice and implement the factors of service leadership. This is dependent upon, first, good leadership skills and, second, the application of service leadership principles.

Four Seasons Hotels

Raised in Toronto, Ontario, Canada, by parents who emigrated from Poland, Isadore Sharp learned the building trade from his father, Max. The Four Seasons hotel eventually grew out of Isadore's initial and successful forays into building and operating hotels. Sharp's business philosophy revolves around the concepts of integrity, trust, and optimism. Being open and honest with his employees engenders trust. Influenced by the Jewish sense of *Tzedakah*, or loving-kindness, inherited from his parents and the long Jewish tradition, this became the bedrock principle of the Four Seasons business.

This is in fact its Golden Rule: Do unto others as you would have them do unto you. For his employees, this translates into being an asset to be enhanced, not a cost to be controlled. For the customers, it translates into a wonderfully personalized experience of service. As a moral understanding the rule is common, but Sharp's leadership makes it uncommon in the details, products, and services provided by the company. Four Seasons operationalizes it as a principle into the details of service taken as a whole. This differentiates Four Seasons from all other luxury hotel brands.

Sharp has stated he used the Golden Rule to form his business and create a corporate culture from top to bottom. All of Four Seasons' brand equity is tied to service excellence. A long list of innovation in service excellence provides ample evidence of Four Seasons' commitment to its founding principle. Service excellence based on this notion of service leadership stands at the core of the value proposition Four Seasons provides its guests, management, and employees. In fact, it has honed processes for ensuring strong execution of this set of values.

Infosys, Bangalore, India

Infosys Limited is a NASDAQ-listed global technology services company headquartered in Bangalore, India. It is the second largest IT exporter in India with more than 160,000 employees. The company specializes in business and technology consulting, application services, systems integration, product engineering, custom software, reengineering, independent testing and validation services, IT infrastructure, and business process outsourcing. Rooted in a Hindu culture, Infosys and its founder believe that the "softest pillow is clear conscience." The values that drive Infosys leadership are customer delight, leadership by example, integrity and transparency, fairness, and the pursuit of excellence.

Infosys from its earliest days has always adopted a sustainable approach to business. Infosys is all about people development. It takes corporate learning more seriously than most companies and invests heavily in it. This was the main vision of the original founders and remains so to this day. The idea of leading at Infosys in spite of enormous company growth, globalization, and demands on its resources is: learning. Using the timeless leadership model of the Bhagavad Gita as a guide, Infosys takes its leaders on a journey. The practical wisdom they come to experience is like no other approach in modern management. The essential guidance applies invincible wisdom, which is governed by intellect, but driven by unselfishness. Discovering the case for righteous action unleashes a notion of work as a means of truly realizing who we are and why we exist. This higher conscious state calms desire and dedicates work to a higher cause.

A leader at Infosys becomes sage. He or she sees the whole as one of aspiration to purpose. In a way, this is paradoxical, as this way of leading is actually an undoing—a state of detached engagement of renunciation in action. Such a form of leadership is ultimately one of self-control, meditative and in constant search for the real self. Mastering the mind is essential, but this discipline takes concentration, detachment, and most of all recognition of transcendence. This sense of stillness found in the Sutras conquers the turbulence of business 24/7. As a spirit-centered leadership, it removes the veil of ego. It liberates those who find it from suffering and stagnation. It also decodes the meaning of life. It sacrifices the smaller for the sake of the greater good. It is about practice as well as eternity. It involves the all-important law of giving, of being and becoming. This is about the character of the leader—not what they do so much as who they are. Infosys is about values, and this shapes their definition and enactment of service leadership.

Tata Group, India

The Tata Group is a multinational conglomerate headquartered in Mumbai, India, and the Tata brand is its most valuable name. Running successful businesses has long been one part of the Tata self-image. Founded in 1868 by the son of a Zoroastrian priest, the company is a service leader that sees itself as a force for modernization and the development of India.

Though the group is a large and profitable business, it sees itself as part of a broader purpose to serve the social welfare of the community wherever it operates. It pursues this service-led purpose in part through its success and its socially responsible business practices. It also pursues it through its primary ownership structure—the Tata Trusts. The stock is held by philanthropic trusts established by former generations of Tata family members. These trusts, whose primary source of income is Tata Group profits, have existed for decades and make millions in grants annually.

Making grants to relieve suffering—from disaster relief to basic health care—their chief goal is related to the Tata companies, building India. In keeping with this service mentality, Tata philanthropy has focused on long-term development projects, typically by making grants to institutional endowments, and Tata's social responsibilities are not restricted to humanitarian projects and the Tata Trusts. Instead, all the Tata companies take a broad view of their corporate purpose, pursuing socially-minded goals in their labor and community relations. The Tata Group's unique character of service and leadership is derived from the ideals of its founder, which in turn owe much of their distinctiveness to the religious culture of his community: the Parsis of western India, who fled Iran to escape persecution for their Zoroastrian faith.

The Maxwell Company

We drew attention to John C. Maxwell, a major *New York Times* bestselling author, coach, and speaker, in Chapter 4. He started off as a full-time pastor in a small church in Ohio and over the years has evolved into the world's foremost leadership expert. He still preaches occasionally at his home church in Florida, and his leadership principles, either explicitly or implied, reflect his Christian worldview. In 2014, he was identified as the number one leader in business by the American Management Association® and the most influential leadership expert in the world by Business Insider and *Inc.* magazine. As the founder of the John Maxwell Company, the John Maxwell Team, EQUIP, and the John Maxwell Leadership Foundation, he has trained more than six million leaders. In 2015, he reached the milestone of having trained leaders from every country in the world. The recipient of the Mother Teresa Prize for Global Peace and Leadership from the Luminary Leadership Network, Dr. Maxwell speaks each year to Fortune 500 companies, presidents of nations, and many of the world's top business leaders. He spoke at the Entrepreneurial Leaders Conference in November 2016 and received the Entrepreneurial Leaders Award.

In terms of his own leadership principles, let us first look at his background. It is surprising that many people seem to be unaware of the role that Christian faith plays in the life of John Maxwell, perhaps because he has become such a prominent mainstream speaker and writer that his past is dwarfed by his present initiatives.

He has spoken out about his faith. He recounts how he started his ministry in a small church in rural Indiana, where the only attendees were himself, his wife, and one other person. He describes how he worked diligently to build up the congregation. The congregation was thriving, and he then moved on to another pastorate. He was disappointed to learn years later that the congregation had dwindled back down to much smaller numbers than when he left. That was one of his first lessons in leadership. It's not about you, but whom you train. He had left no leaders to carry the torch. While he got his start in the ministry, what about the present? John Maxwell is also quick to point out that he is currently a teaching pastor for Christ Fellowship Church, Palm Beach Gardens, Florida.

While John Maxwell maintains a preaching ministry, what led to his focus on leadership training? Well, on July 4, 1976, while he was leading a service celebrating the US bicentennial, he says, "I got a sense that God was calling me to help other Christian leaders to grow and reach their potential for the cause of Christ."[20] This started his thirty-plus-year career helping others learn about leadership, in the Christian community and beyond. Maxwell believes in the importance of leadership, especially for Christians: "Make your aim to practice transformational leadership, where people's lives are changed from the inside out. That kind of leadership is based on character, conviction, and Christlikeness. In other words, transformational leadership follows the patterns laid down in Scriptures."

His desire to train others led him to begin writing books on the topic. As his books gained traction, he also received more speaking opportunities. He also started various faith-related initiatives such as the INJOY Life Club and EQUIP. Some of his books are more overtly Christian than others. For example, *Be All You Can Be: A Challenge to Stretch Your God-given Potential* (2007) is the product of the leadership lessons he gave to staff at Skyline Wesleyan Church in San Diego, where he pastored from 1981 to 1995. He refers to many biblically sourced lessons. Maxwell states that "What makes a person extraordinary is purpose—the consuming desire to accomplish something in life." In Maxwell's opinion, the great leaders in the Bible were called to live their calling. Likewise, Maxwell maintains that same divine motivation for intentional living.

In his most recent book, *Intentional Living: Choosing a Life That Matters* (2015), Maxwell says, "I talk pretty openly about my faith in this book. I do that because it has been an important part of my personal journey." The point of the book is not to proselytize, but to have people think about their life purpose. John Maxwell always

20 Richard J. Goossen meeting with John C. Maxwell, Vancouver, BC, Canada, Jan 3, 2017.

emphasizes that leadership needs to be lived first—then taught. How does he do it? In *Intentional Living*, he explains that

> God helps to make my best, as flawed as it is, even better. I have always believed that God will be there for me and help me. In fact, my belief in myself grows out of my faith. I totally embrace the words in Jeremiah 29:11—"For I know the plans I have for you" declares the Lord, "plans to prosper you and not to harm you, plans to give you hope and a future."

In *Intentional Living*, he also notes that "There is only one thing in my life that I value more than intentional living in order to achieve significances, and that is God. He can do more than I can imagine, guess, or dream about" (p. 71). John Maxwell has had a great influence in both the larger Christian community and the mainstream leadership world—from the unlikely beginnings in a small church in rural Indiana.

National Bank of Kuwait

Islamic banking and finance (IBF) is considered the most developed part of Islamic economics. IBF is more complex than just interest-free banking. Along with the prohibition of *riba* (usury), *ghara* (speculation), and *haram* (forbidden products), IBF has a number of other characteristics. Risk is shared by terms of financial transactions, in a symmetrical risk/return distribution. All financial transactions are directly linked to an underlying economic transaction. This means that options and other derivatives are banned. Restrictions on exploitation are taken seriously. No party to any banking transaction can be exploited or oppressed. These may seem to Westerners at least to be large restrictions, yet IBF has grown very rapidly in much of the Islamic world. The assets of IBF are estimated by the *Economist* to be in excess of $2 trillion dollars, and the practices can be found in more than seventy countries today. The trend has been growing steadily over the last two decades.

National Bank of Kuwait (NBK) is an example of an IBF-oriented institution. The bank is the largest player in its market with regards to assets and deposits, more than twice as large as its next biggest rival, Gulf Bank. Founded in 1952 as the first local bank and first shareholding company in the Gulf region, NBK has since grown to develop a large international network in 16 countries. It has 155 branches in New York, London, and Paris and throughout the entire Middle East.

The bank was named the "best bank" in the region and has earned the highest credit ratings from Standard & Poor's. They have an AA- from Fitch Ratings and an Aa3 from Moody's. The bank has grown to be both competitive and highly appreciated by its clients. The reason for its success is its clear Islamic orientation and keeping to those standards.

According to Isam Al-Sager, Group Chief Executive at NBK, the future of banking is right now. The NBK has set out:

- To be the premier Arab Bank.
- To achieve consistently superior return for our shareholders.
- To deliver world-class products and services to our customers.
- To invest in people.
- To benefit the communities in which we operate.

The NBK is unique in that it is almost wholly privately owned, unlike the vast majority of other banks in Kuwait and in the Middle East. The leadership model at NBK is truly and authentically Islamic, and it follows and adheres to the tenets of the faith on economics. This has not made it unprofitable. The relative stability of the bank even through the recent financial crisis suggests that IBF serves as a strong foundation on which to build and establish credible financial institutions. The principles of Islamic banking are becoming more of an economic reality and a favorable one in terms of prudent behavior and integrity. This is an important trend and another non-Western example of how leadership determines service according to a faith-based tradition with implications for practice and reputation.

CHAPTER 8

SERVICE LEADERSHIP: PERSONAL IMPACT

Service Leadership Markers

    6. Job Fit

    7. Passion and Creative Expression

    8. Facilitate the Pursuit of Excellence

    9. Personal Connection to the Whole

    10. Autonomy

    11. Serving

    12. Listening and Respect

Conclusion

As noted in previous chapters, "Service Leadership" can be defined by the following general/corporate and specific/personal "markers." By "markers," we mean defining characteristics that reflect our concept of service leadership. The general/corporate markers comprise the framework set by the company. The specific/personal factors relate to the particular role of the individual in any given company. Next, we'll look at these markers in more detail.

SERVICE LEADERSHIP MARKERS

6. JOB FIT

This first marker is referred to simply as "job fit." We believe that unless the right person is in the right job, he or she will not be able to find meaningful work. If this is he case, there will be aggravation on both sides: the employer will have someone who is not performing adequately, and the individual will not believe that he or she is living up to his or her potential. How does a company achieve the right fit? The best companies take a long time to hire and are quick to fire; not the reverse. The better the company, typically the more rigorous is the selection and interview process. There are many practical tools for achieving fit: detailed job descriptions; multiple interviewers and multiple stages; and comprehensive psychological assessment tests that measure such fit. We will now look at some companies that strive to achieve a good job fit for their employees.

Safe Software

Finding employees who are a good fit for an organization is not always an easy process, regardless of how much effort goes into the process. When there is not a good fit, it is a disappointment to both the company and the individual selected. As Dale Lutz, Safe Software's cofounder, shares,

The thing that I find the hardest is when things don't work out with staff members. To have to let someone go is one of the hardest things to do. We've had to do that many times now over the years. Not as many as some other companies, but nonetheless, more than I would ever have wanted to.[21]

As the cliché goes, any business leader who enjoys any part of letting someone go should not be in leadership. Lutz explains:

I know that a necessary part of being an entrepreneur is to have to look someone in the eyeballs and make that hard decision to end the relationship. But if you highly value relationships with people, if you value your staff immensely, to have to let someone go, no matter what the reason —even if you know it's the right thing, even if you know that for both parties it will be happier afterwards, which incidentally has always been the case—it's still very hard.

In some cases, this will involve friends—and this can make the dynamics much more complicated. Lutz explains one scenario:

I reflect on one individual who was really a good friend of mine and after many years it was clear to us that it just wasn't working—for him or for the company. We had the hard talk and we parted ways. A very rewarding experience for me was that about nine months later we got together for lunch and he told me his story of how much happier he ended up being by not working with us. We didn't realize the magnitude of both parties' unhappiness. Sometimes making a hard decision is the right thing but it's still a really tough thing to do.

---

21 This quotation and all the others from Dale Lutz in this section are taken from a personal interview between Richard J. Goossen and Dale Lutz, Vancouver, BC.

How then can a business owner work toward getting the right fit with employees? Lutz explains his approach to the process:

> I think the development of a normative approach around dealing with employees is a big issue. People—all of us—are flawed. I am flawed and sometimes employees are flawed. You put some of those flaws together and there will be situations that aren't easy and so reconciling that and having the strength to recognize when you are at fault and having a low enough ego yourself to accept it. At the same time—when others are at fault—you need to be able to work through that.

So, we can work to try to achieve a fit, but we always realize that we are flawed and that despite our best efforts it may not work out.

IM Group

Robert Edmiston, Baron Edmiston, has a one-of-a-kind faith and entrepreneurial journey. He started his career as a bank clerk, but as an entrepreneur Edmiston achieved success through IM Group, a car importer, and IM Properties. His son, Andrew Edmiston, now manages IM Group. In the [London] *Sunday Times* Rich List 2013 ranking of the wealthiest people in the UK, Robert Edmiston was placed 209th with an estimated net worth of £440 million. A committed Christian who has donated approximately £180 million to charities, in 1988, Edmiston and his wife, Tracie, founded Christian Vision (CV). CV is an international charity with offices in 22 countries working to support the Christian church in the areas of evangelism and discipleship in both the online and offline space. CV makes full use of media platforms to spread the Good News in the entire world. Edmiston's vision is to reach a billion people with the gospel. Created a life peer with the title Baron Edmiston in 2011, he served in the House of Lords until 2015. He is also the principal sponsor of three City Academy schools in the West Midlands region of the UK.

Lord Edmiston is accustomed to building an organization by getting good people and transitioning out those who are not a fit. He recounted that once his business started to grow, dealing with people was one of the most difficult problems. He explains,

> As the business grows you overtake some people's capabilities and you have to deal with that. That is difficult and sensitive, particularly if those people have been loyal and stuck with you for years. Suddenly you are saying, "you are no longer the appropriate person for the job."[22]

How to deal with this is a significant challenge. Lord Edmiston explains that

> We make enough money that we can afford to carry a little bit of fat, but when a recession comes along you can't afford to carry any fat and then that becomes really difficult. Some of these people have been with us a long time.

He further provides a specific example:

> I think about our computer manager, for instance. He was stuck in a different age with big main frames and he had to go. He had been with me for 35 years. He was due to retire so we came up with a package, but he has gone and is still a bit bitter and that is sad. I didn't want that but it was the right thing to do, we had to cut costs. We saved about £2 million in the computer department. It had just grown fat and was inefficient. Instead of buying off-the-shelf solutions we had built everything on what we had started 30 years previous. It had been layer upon layer and every time you wanted to change this you had to change

---

22 Richard J. Goossen interview with Robert Edmiston, Vancouver, BC, Canada, November 5, 2015.

the whole structure. So there were much better solutions around but mentally he wasn't capable of grasping that.

Clearly a decision needed to be made, as there was no longer a fit between the person and the position.

In terms of looking for a good fit, what were the key attributes Edmiston looked for in people (partners, advisors, managers) as he grew the company? He summarized his position as "Character, competence, and loyalty." He explains,

> I don't like people who just jumped around here, there, and everywhere. In the first few years of your career it is reasonable to jump, but when you are a senior executive you don't want to be changing jobs every three or four years. Personal recommendations are often really good, but not always.

Phantom Screens

Esther de Wolde is President of Phantom Screens, Canada. De Wolde describes her business:

> At Phantom, we have the fun of pioneering a new industry. Today, we are considered part of what is called the "fenestration" industry [fenestration relates to the design and placement of openings, such as windows and doors, in the building envelope]. Since we began, we have spent loads of money to create awareness not only at the consumer level, but also at the builder influencer level (i.e., architects, builders, and designers). Hopefully one day soon, we will have our own screening category within the construction industry.[23]

---

23 Dallas Froese interview with Esther de Wolde, June 23, 2008, in Richard J. Goossen, ed, *Entrepreneurial Leaders: Reflections on Faith At Work.* Langley, BC: Trinity Western University, 2008.

De Wolde explains how the company had evolved:

> As we grew, we began to realize that we weren't selling screens as much as we were creating comfort, space and preserving views within our customer's homes. To hear our customers' testimonials, you would never think they are talking about a screen. It never gets boring for us to hear about their personal "Phantom experience."

When asked about the strength of her business, she responded:

> And, today, as it was in the beginning, I believe one of our greatest strengths is to understand and embrace the "people" side of our business. We want to ensure that our people are on the right bus in the right seats (thank you Jim Collins[24]) and feel respected and valued, no matter what position they hold within Phantom.

When asked about the most important lessons she had learned with respect to starting and running a business to pass on to an aspiring entrepreneur, she responds: "It's all about the people. That's the most critical piece to me. You need an appreciation for people in general, hiring for attitude, not aptitude, that whole concept. Treat them right and they will treat you right."

Auntie Anne's Pretzels

Anne Beiler built a global pretzel business. She has an amazing story of entrepreneurial success, going from a small town farmer's

---

24 Jim Collins discusses this concept in his best-selling book *From Good to Great*, 2005.

market to the world of international franchising. She explained the beginnings:

> When I first started, the product itself really grew the company. In our first year [1988] we went from the one store to a second store within the first year [1989]. The following year [1990] we built 10 stores and we did all of that under a licensing agreement. We didn't realize at the time that we were actually franchising because I didn't know anything about franchising. People came to us after they tasted the product. Word began to spread in our little community and into Philadelphia, New York and down the east coast. People would come and ask us if they could sell our pretzels. I realized that we needed to have some form of agreement, so we called it a licensing agreement.[25]

How did the opportunity come up? Anne explained what happened:

> First, I worked for someone at a farmer's market for 7 months. At that particular store, we had a number of items and I convinced the owner of the store I was managing that the pretzel is the key product and can I please exclude everything else that we're selling. It took me a while but eventually we just did pretzels at that store because that was the moneymaker. I then had an opportunity to buy my own store in a nearby farmer's market. At that store, again, they had pretzels. To identify the opportunity and the product for me was easy—the opportunity right in front of my face. I didn't go out looking for it.

She lists one of the strengths of the business as her people: "the pretzel caused us to hire the best people in the world—in our community,

---

25 Richard J. Goossen interview with Anne Beiler by phone, January 27, 2011.

I should say." What were the key attributes she looked for in people? She explains her process. First, "we always talked about a teachable spirit. Whether a person was going to work from a home office or were going to become franchisees, they had to have a teachable spirit." Second, "We looked for people who had a good work ethic." Last, "We looked for people who could buy into our purpose and our mission." Anne also notes that "It wasn't important for them to have a lot of education or even be very wealthy people. The "fit" is most important.

Of course, not everyone is a fit. Beiler explains her experience dealing with this situation, as well:

> We had some very, very good experiences, which, to this day, have been amazingly positive. They still have their franchises and they are doing very well. There are others that turned out negatively because they didn't want to comply with the Auntie Anne's standards. They thought they could do it their own way. At the end of the day, however, I feel like I was able to talk all of those issues out with any of those that I had differences with. But, that was really up to me to do. As far as I know, I haven't burned any bridges.

So, we see that establishing the proper fit can be engineered successfully with some deft handling.

NovaQuest

NovaQuest is a private equity firm focused on life sciences. Gerry Brown, the chairman of the UK-based firm, has a long experience with some of the largest providers of biopharmaceutical developments and outsourcing services over many decades.

NovaQuest was created as a spinout from Quintiles. The investors included such giant private equity investors as Bain Capital,

Temasek, TPG, and 3i. Japanese companies were also anchor investors, primarily through Mitsui Bank. The company focuses on pharmaceutical products that are in late-stage clinical development or have entered into commercialization.

As a niche player, the company invests considerable funds in specific and very specialized products. NovaQuest helps big pharma companies facing the so-called patent cliff (simultaneous expiration of patents on existing drugs) by sharing the risks from long and expensive development processes. NovaQuest invests not so much in equity in companies as primarily in the products of those companies. The company is skilled at helping companies benchmark their work and make better decisions about prioritizing the products to take forward in development. Building these pipelines is critical to success in biopharmaceuticals. As a global company, NovaQuest also has access to the expertise in every stage of development from clinical trials to marketing and distribution. This is its advantage and true value.

The big issue for such a company, according to Gerry Brown, is "building a team." The company had a lot of experience in the field, including with private equity houses. It had financial rigor and the skills needed to make decisive investments. It had the infrastructure of a global company. But it lacked the teamwork necessary to execute its mission. It had to learn how to get to financial directors first and ahead of the logical discussions with R&D directors. Inevitably, the company experienced a number of cultural issues, some having to do with values and culture, others with the bias and focus on America and, to a limited extent, Japan.

The lessons learned, according to Brown, revolve around the role and task of leadership and the role of the all-important independent directors. Working with the board of directors was critical for NovaQuest. The first lesson was to get on the same page as regards strategy. Strategy determines most things in pharmaceuticals. The second lesson was to get the essential experience of professionals on board.

This industry is especially complex, and it is important to know how to navigate all the regulations and build relationships with key investors. Brown spelled out the need for a more effective way to guide this process and an effective board presence in his book, *The Independent Director* (Brown, 2015).

NovaQuest found that to be a leader in its chosen domain, it needed both managers and board members with a wide range of experience, varied backgrounds and skills, and a variety of perspectives that led to dialogue, debate, and consideration of many options.

The idea of diversity here is cast very wide. The independent directors at NovaQuest are not seen to work in isolation. Rather, they are part of a team that has responsibility for governing and steering the whole organization. These leaders need to give service to the mission of the firm and not to their own whims and fancies.

Boards today are very demanding. They must consider a wide array of ethical and governance issues that could potentially have an adverse effect on the company and its stakeholders, according to Brown. This leads boards to seek out both directors and managers of the business who are committed and who follow best practices. They need to engage both their boards and managers for the larger purpose of the company. Getting this right makes all the difference, especially in a business as challenging a global biopharma.

7. PASSION AND CREATIVE EXPRESSION

Another factor of service leadership is to facilitate the creative expression of individuals. Even though organizations need to have uniformity in their training, systems, and procedures, there still can, and needs to, be some room for creative expression, to tap into the passion of the individual. This is an important aspect of facilitating the pursuit of meaning for individuals. Izzo and Klein (1997, p. 58), cited earlier, note that "when people know their own passions, when their work is an outgrowth of that passion, and when their personal values live through their work—energy flows and commitment grows." This creative expression can take place in various forms.

This is the opportunity for individuals to use their primary and secondary skills so that they feel that they are using their abilities to the utmost. In a practical sense, this means giving people some scope for creative expression. Amortegui (2014) refers to "job crafting" as a tool that empowers people to think through their role by using three well-researched meaning frames: coupling, decoupling, or rearranging tasks; reformulating social interactions; and simply fine-tuning the perception of the purpose of your work. Amortegui (2014) concludes:

> In the end, you emerge with greater clarity on how to retrofit your job to your unique passions, values, and strengths. The most successful and fulfilled at work are relentless job crafters. They are able to use the raw material afforded in their work to mold more meaning. In doing so, they find ways to give their best selves in service of what others need—a critical meaning-making ingredient

We'll now look at the following companies as further examples: More Than Just Great Dancing, Covenant, and Google.

More Than Just Dancing, USA

Misty Lown is a dynamic entrepreneur with a unique and inspiring story. She is the founder, president, and energized force behind More Than Just Great Dancing™, a licensed dance studio affiliation program that has a positive impact on over fifty thousand dance students around the globe each week.[26] She is also the founder of www.MoreThanDancers.com, an online lifestyle magazine for young people that has over 50,000 visitors each month. Born with a clubfoot

---

26 See www.mistylown.com.

and a survivor of an eating disorder, Misty Lown is an unlikely candidate to be a professional dancer and studio owner, but audiences around the world enjoy the grace and grit with which Misty tells her entrepreneurial story and the lessons it provides for the dance of life.

Misty's Dance Unlimited, founded in 1998 in the USA and named as one of the "Top 50 Studios in the Nation" by *Dance Spirit Magazine*, has provided $225,000 in scholarship for dancers. Misty has been a speaker at the PULSE Teachers Convention, Hollywood Connection, Dance Teacher Web, Dance Teacher Summit, and the DanceLife Conference. She has also been the keynote speaker for the Australian Teachers of Dancing Convention. Misty is on the staff of Dance Revolution Convention, a faith-based dance convention, and has written over forty industry articles.

Misty is an entrepreneur at heart. In addition to her dance studio and licensing program, she owns a dancewear store, a dance competition, and a self-storage business. She is the author of the book *More Than Business* and creator of the IamMORE podcast. Describing herself as having "entrepreneurial attention deficit disorder," Misty has taken the best of her business ventures to the top of her industry while taking the lessons from the failures to heart. Misty's favorite part of the day is spending time with her husband and five children.

Misty explained that

I have followed the call to take the work I do with students locally to start a global movement that now has a direct positive impact on 53,000 children in dance each week through our 148 affiliate schools in the US, Canada, Australia, Aruba and Dubai. We recently launched an associated online magazine that has had over a half million visits in the last six months from 96 countries. It's not what I thought I would do with my life, but it's better.[27]

27 Richard J. Goossen conversation with Misty Lown, Toronto, Canada, November 16, 2016.

But why licensing rather than franchising? The concepts are indeed quite different. The franchising approach is to provide a business opportunity along with a business format. There are very strict guidelines from the franchisor on how to run the business, the product, the format, the uniforms, the pricing, and the like. Further, the offering is a set business format—and cannot be combined with other offerings. The franchisor is looking for franchisees to implement a proven business format but in a new part of town. Well-known franchises include McDonald's and many other fast food chains; franchising also exists in many other business spheres. Licensing, which is Misty Lown's approach, is different. Licensing involves the use of specific products or systems, but with flexibility as to how those particular products or services are integrated into existing offerings. For example, there may be a small coffee shop on a university campus that is offering Starbucks coffee; it will have a Starbucks logo and sell Starbucks coffee, but in the context of a standard-issue non-descript coffee shop.

Misty determined that the better approach for her to expand was to provide a licensing opportunity. This would provide the individual dance studios with an opportunity to benefit from the use of Misty's unique material but not be restricted from using their own creative concepts. In this context, this allows for a better relationship between the two parties and ensures more ongoing collaboration.

Covenant Family Wealth Advisors

Covenant Family Wealth Advisors is a Canadian boutique firm focused on succession and transition strategies for high net worth individuals. There is a team of about twenty individuals. There are a handful of relationship managers who source and build relationships with high net worth family business owners and entrepreneurs throughout Canada. The firm provides will and estate planning, business success / transition services, and philanthropic counsel. A related company offers wealth management.

Covenant provides an excellent example of a firm that practices service leadership and, in particular, allows for creative expression by its professionals. As part of the firm, a relationship manager has a specific job description and performance criteria. The relationship manager is hired for certain skill sets. Yet, at the same time, there is great autonomy in how the relationship manager delivers results. For example, an important part of the duties of the relationship manager is business development. The relationship manager then works with the firm's marketing manager, who is there to support whatever initiatives she thinks are useful rather than to somehow constrain the relationship manager.

The relationship managers will engage in the following activities: They will devise information tools, such as a Practice Bulletin, to distribute to clients. They will create and organize a seminar presentation, attract panelists, and market the event. They will be invited to various business functions to make a presentation. They can determine which events they would like to attend where they might meet people interested in the firm's services. In all of the above activities, relationship managers have the opportunity to exercise some creative expression. They are not explicitly hired to do the above things, but they are activities that help them fulfil the purposes of Covenant. The relationship managers experience greater work satisfaction, since they have an opportunity to exercise more of the abilities these individuals have to offer.

Google

Google is well known in the press for its innovative practices, including its 70:20:10 rule. This rule means that 70 percent of each employee's time should be spent on core business, 20 percent on projects related to that core, and 10 percent on projects not related to core business. Engineers are entitled and expected to use time for their own projects according to the 20 percent rule. When employees in other units have ideas that they wish to develop, they are most often given the freedom to realize their ideas or the ideas of others—again, according to the 20 percent rule. This project-oriented activity is carried out in parallel to daily operations. At Google, each employee's performance is valued according to both the aspects of production and innovation.

8. FACILITATE THE PURSUIT OF EXCELLENCE

Another important component of service leadership is the pursuit of excellence. The vast majority of people find it meaningful to be part of doing something great, pursuing it with excellence, and being rewarded or recognized directly or indirectly. This is why people celebrate championship teams and companies that have invented new products. In this section, we will refer to various companies that give examples of the pursuit of excellence. Pink defines mastery as "the desire to get better and better at something that matters."

This book referred earlier to Paul J. Zak on the neuroscience of trust and how that is related to meaningful work. Zak notes that neuroscience shows that a company facilitates excellence through recognition: "Public recognition not only uses the power of the crowd to celebrate successes, but also inspires others to aim for excellence. And it gives top performers a forum for sharing best practices, so others can learn from them."

We will look at some examples of companies that have inspired employees to aim for excellence.

Auntie Anne's Pretzels

One of the things that Anne Beiler, whom we met earlier, found to be most personally rewarding and satisfying as an entrepreneur was to watch people grow into excellence over time. Beiler explains:

> I love watching people grow. People spent different amounts of time with Auntie Anne's; they'd be there for maybe a year,

some are still there to this day, some have been there almost as long as the company has existed. It was very satisfying for me to see people go from being unprofessional and unfocused and then becoming a VP of a particular department or whatever. That could happen because they were in an environment where we rewarded people that were productive. We would send them to workshops. We were very deliberate about people growing.[28]

Martinrea International

The pursuit of excellence is important for Martinrea Inc, a company with 15,000 employees and with plants all over the world. One of the core values of Martinrea is "We make great, high quality products." Rob Wildeboer, Executive Chairman and cofounder, whom we met in Chapter 7, explains that

> Nothing should detract from this, and if we don't we will not survive or be No. 1. That is what it is all about—not buying companies, not being the biggest, not being the cheapest, not being the fastest growing but being the best. Quality really is the basis of job security and opportunity for our people. We are good in many areas, great in some, but there is always room to improve (Wildeboer, 2015b).

Another core value is that "Every plant/division must be a center of excellence." Wildeboer explains,

> Not a center of adequacy, but excellence. Some of our plants are, we believe, the best in the world in what they do: Saltillo for fluids, Queretaro and Madrid for aluminum blocks and structures; some of our metallics plants consistently win supplier awards (Wildeboer, 2015b).

---

28 Beiler Interview.

Excellence is inspiring and motivating; employees feel much better about this undertaking than being in a state of mediocrity.

Toyota

Toyota is a Japanese company that follows the values of the Shinto tradition, which emphasizes the pursuit of excellence in all areas. Sakichi Toyoda was an inventor and industrialist who founded Toyota Industries Co. Born in 1867, in Kosai, Japan, Dr. Toyoda was the son of a poor carpenter, but he became known as the father of the Japanese industrial revolution. By inventing devices and most famously the automatic power loom, he applied his principles of *jidoka* ("intelligent automation") to both problem solving and manufacturing. His principles became a central component of the Toyota production system. Toyoda left a legacy that infuses the leadership, management principles, and operational philosophy that continues to this day. His descendants have comprised much of the leadership of the Toyota Motor Company founded in 1937.

The spirit of leadership at Toyota, now one of the world's largest automotive manufacturers, is best encapsulated by an understanding of the Toyota Production System. This system pervades the company and colors its views on social responsibility and sustainable development, all of which grow out of Japanese Shinto traditions. As such, Toyota has long engaged in business with the idea of corporate social responsibility in mind. The company has used internal working groups and other bodies to investigate in-depth means of responding to societal demands . . . believing that by putting into practice the spirit of the Guiding Principles at Toyota, the company is fulfilling society's expectation of Toyota.

Our interviews at Toyota underscored the way in which the Toyota Production System contributes to the culture and spirit of the company. That integrated sociotechnical system organizes manufacturing and logistics, including interaction with suppliers and customers. The main objectives are to design out overburden or stress to the system. By removing inconsistencies and eliminating waste, the company in essence can process the aims to rid itself of *mura* and embrace flexibility.

The service orientation at Toyota underlies what is called the Toyota Way, which underpins its managerial approach and entire production system. The principles of continuous improvement include the desire to establish a long-term vision, tackle challenges, and, most critically, innovate. The principle also pertains to respect for people and includes building teamwork.

Toyota is a global but still thoroughly Japanese company with a definitive culture and a service production philosophy that dates all the way back to its founder. The Toyota Way and continuous improvement is not just a mantra at Toyota; it is a defining and comprehensive system. It is ingrained in the code of conduct and in the global vision of the company.

9. PERSONAL CONNECTION TO THE WHOLE

An important determinant of meaning in work is for the employee to understand his or her connection to the whole. The performance of a mundane task may be boring, debilitating, and utterly devoid of meaning—but a connection to the bigger picture can change all that.

Robert Edmiston

Robert Edmiston, referred to earlier, gives an apt example of the impact of this type of thinking in relation to his company's giving:

> It is no secret I am a Christian. My employees know that. They know I give money to Christian charity. One of the attractions for people to come and work for me is that I am not just using the money for myself. My employees can see that we are actually doing something good. It's like the

story about the three builders. Each was asked what he was doing. The first said "I am laying bricks." The next said "I am building this wall." The third guy said "I am building a cathedral." They were all doing the same thing but they each had a different perspective on what they were doing. I like that people have a bigger perspective. From our company we are sending trips to Cambodia and people from across the company go, we raise money, gals are baking cakes, one guy is losing two stones of weight, and so on.

This connection to the whole can happen in various ways, but the key is that the individual can link their specific activities to a greater purpose.

Amortegui points out the value of the big picture:

Consider one computer manufacturer's mission statement: "To be the most successful computer company in the world." That's great. But it displays a major meaning trap that many of us fall prey to—it's all about us. What if the mission statement read: "To be the most successful computer company *for* the world"? Meaning comes when we realize the impact of our work on others. In fact, what distinguishes the most successful givers—versus those who burn out—is not what or how much they give. It is that they know the difference they make to others. People aren't inspired solely by what they do. People are lit up when they know why what they do matters.

In the relentless grind of our daily work, we often forget the positive and enduring impact our work has on others.

Daniel Pink talks about organizations becoming "purpose maximizers." He talks about ways in which employees are motivated and how present systems don't work well in many respects. He points out in *Drive* that we're intrinsically motivated purpose maximizers, not only extrinsically motivated profit maximizers. It doesn't comport with the way that twenty-first-century economics thinks about what we do—because economists are finally realizing that we're full-fledged human beings, not single-minded economic robots (Pink, p. 31).

Organizations need to understand that employees are not motivated solely by economic incentives. Instead, they should realize that they are dealing with integrated individuals who have a range of motivations. The present system is based on "contingent rewards"—if you do this, then you'll get that. Pink points out that this approach often has a negative effect—because people forfeit some of their autonomy (p. 36). As discussed elsewhere, intrinsic motivation is far more important than extrinsic motivation. Pink elaborates further that "For routine tasks, which aren't very interesting and don't demand much creative thinking, rewards can provide a small motivational booster shot without the harmful side effects" (Pink, p. 60). But this motivation doesn't work for higher-level, creative tasks. Pink's perspective is that for motivating people, "The essential requirement: *Any extrinsic reward should be unexpected and offered only after the task is complete*" (ibid., p. 64).

Pink is an advocate for "Self-Determination Theory," which argues that people have three innate psychological needs: competence, autonomy, and relatedness (ibid., p. 70). He explains that "Human beings have an innate inner drive to be autonomous, self-determined, and connected to one another. And when that drive is liberated, people achieve more and live richer lives" (ibid., p. 71). He describes a theory of motivations. He differentiates between "Theory X," which is belief in the mediocrity of the masses, and "Theory Y," which is belief in the potential of people (ibid., p. 74). He suggests moving away from these two theories and instead using "Type I" (note that this is not related to the Approach that we identify as Type I in this book). Pink explains that

Ultimately, Type I behavior depends on three nutrients: autonomy, mastery, and purpose. Type I behavior is self-directed. It is devoted to becoming better and better at something that matters. And it connects that quest for excellence to a larger purpose (ibid., pp. 78–79).

Adventurer Group

In order to discover how individual performance links to the big picture of a company, let us introduce James Epp and his company. He has spent almost 50 years perfecting and expanding his niche. He owns and operates Adventurer Group, the largest recreational vehicle (RV) company in Canada. James's story has one main lesson for other entrepreneurs—there are no shortcuts to success.

While the media loves quick "overnight" success stories, a more common tale from the entrepreneurial front is that of founders who painstakingly building companies over decades. The process involves learning hard lessons in the marketplace, making careful strategic moves, constantly pursuing incremental and large scale innovation, and embedding in the business ecosystem as delivering a valuable product that consumers will pay for—and surviving through the ebb and flow of the marketplace.

That's precisely how James Epp has built Adventurer Group. Over almost fifty years, James and his entrepreneurial family grew this business to over seven hundred employees and thirteen dealerships across Canada, plus an RV manufacturing company in Yakima, Washington. James first started in the RV business as a raw teenager when his father, Erdman, purchased a camper manufacturing business in 1969, which came with five employees. He started in the company during high school by sweeping floors and taking out garbage and then working the assembly line. He worked full-time in the summer and twenty-hour weeks during the school year, getting increasingly involved at different levels over the course of the company's growth. James often jokes that instead of postsecondary education, he attended his father Erdman's "School of Business."

So, over an almost fifty-year period, the Adventurer Group has grown from modest origins to encompass five different brands (Fraserway RV, Country RV, Four Seasons RV Rentals, Roadmaster RV, and Travelhome RV) that make up 13 dealerships across Canada. The Group also has a manufacturing plant, which builds the Adventurer, Eagle Cap, and Okanagan brands. There is a rentals division with 1,300 units on fleet. The company also has a parts retail unit sales and wholesale distribution under the brand Specialty RV Products.

In addition to the operational divisions, James also established the Adventurer Foundation, which supports extensive charitable activities. James's eyes light up at the prospect of being able to support a range of worthwhile causes. Employees are involved, too, such as collectively sponsoring hundreds of needy children in Kenya since 2005.

So, what are James's insights into connecting individual performance to the whole? First, James has built a devoted team, from management and staff. He cares about his extended team and treats them well—they clearly want to work for him. There are many long-term employees. He often walks the premises and chats with everyone, from salespeople to those in the service department. Often when asked how he managed to build such a large and diverse company, James clearly states that God has blessed him over the years with many great managers and employees. James has successfully invested in the human infrastructure as a platform for growth.

Second, they have very clear company values and keep reinforcing them—and reflect them to all the staff. The company is rooted in core values regarding employees, customers, integrity, respect, workplace, teamwork, recreation, innovation, community, social action, and biblical principles. These values are founded in James's belief system. They are displayed in all the offices—and employees are expected to act accordingly.

Third, the company has a very committed senior management team. The senior executives have both intrinsic and extrinsic motivations. On the extrinsic side, there is a carefully constructed bonus system that is tied to the revenue and profits of the organization. There are also the perks that come with being part of a successful organization. On the intrinsic side, there are the motivations of being part of the leading company in Canada in its field, providing great service to many satisfied customers and contributing to the greater good that the company is doing through its charitable activities.

Michelin

Michelin is a well-known global brand, especially in tires, founded in France in 1889 by the brothers Michelin, who took over a rubber ball factory that had opened in Clermont-Ferrand in 1832. From manufacturing tires for bicycles and horse-drawn carriages, within a decade Michelin began to manufacture tires for cars and developed pneumatic tires. To promote tourism by car, the company began publishing in 1900 travel guides for automotive travelers, listing towns large enough to have gas stations, repair garages, hotels, and restaurants. As the automotive market grew rapidly, Michelin came to be synonymous with tires for everything from trucks to cars to bicycles to planes. Over time, the company expanded plants all over Europe. Early on, the company developed rubber plantations in Asia. In 1990, Michelin acquired the Uniroyal-Goodrich Tire Company, becoming the largest tire company in the world.

Michelin has always been a family concern and every leader has been a descendant of the founder Edouard. The company has a unique leadership and governance structure, which is independent and able to prevent possible takeover attempts. With a strong Roman Catholic orientation around ethics and guiding principles, Michelin is unapologetic about applying those principles in the company. To quote a former CEO, " Christian faith . . . explains why the world is ordered as it is. It shows the basic attitude that we should have in order to grow and to help others grow." This has led to an emphasis on individual growth potential, which is fundamental to Michelin's beliefs. By helping its workers reach toward the limitless potential that Michelin believes key to each individual, the company throughout its long history has sought to find the contribution that each person can make. In the words of their human resources director, "the company must find the means to make it possible for each person's predominant trait to be brought out. It must also give each person the opportunity to become what he/she is."

This respect for each person's potential reflects the philosophy of the company founder who reportedly told his managers, "your number one task is love the employees for whom you are responsible." The company believes they must do so, as all workers, no matter how small their task, were "accomplishing a work of craft." This has proven to ameliorate any tensions between workers and managers and to solve problems not by enforcing a rigid bureaucracy, but by making sure all employees understand the goals and the culture of the company. This understanding of freedom and accountability has colored Michelin's activities down the years.

Responsible leadership at Michelin today is structured into its charter called Michelin Performance and Responsibility. The document established a formal framework of five core values that define the company's responsibilities to its stakeholders, with the goal of clearly stating those values to ensure their implementation. Those core values are:

Respect for people;
Respect for customers;
Respect for shareholders;
Respect for the environment; and
Respect for facts.

Underpinning these values is the belief stated by the founder, "we have one profession and one mission: contribute to the long-run progress in the field of mobility."

Analysis of the service model at Michelin is inseparable from analysis of the personal ethics grafted into the company by its founder. This is, in its own terms, "an active and unapologetic Catholic" way that is applied to the company and its public life. The leadership model rooted in respect advocates providing an opportunity for people to discover their true strengths and interests, to be the best people they can become, and to operate within an environment of shared trust and deep respect.

10. AUTONOMY

Another important component of the practice of service leadership is the concept of autonomy. This is somewhat ironic: a person joins a company and voluntarily submits to selling his or her time and expertise but at the same time wants a certain amount of independence from that same company. Autonomy means some control over the process of getting things done as contrasted with direction on what to do, when to do it by, and what it should look like. This is a very important part of meaning, as people want to have some self-control that matches their preferred pace of work, work environment, and means of getting something done. As Pink notes in *Drive*, "It means acting with choice—which means we can be both autonomous and happily interdependent with others" (p. 88). In other words, there is a difference between being "dependent" and "interdependent." There are creative benefits to an organization from crafting this type of work environment. Pink notes that "A sense of autonomy has a powerful effect on individual performance and attitude," adding, "Autonomy over task has long been critical to their [employees'] ability to create" (ibid.).

The neuroeconomist Zak notes that one of the factors in creating a high trust environment is "Give people discretion in how they do their work." In other words, give employees a high degree of autonomy. Once employees have been trained, allow them to execute a project at their own discretion. Zak explains that "Being trusted to figure things out is a big motivator: A 2014 Citigroup and LinkedIn survey found that nearly half of employees would give up a 20 percent raise for greater control over how they work." The bottom line, according to Zak, is that

> Autonomy also promotes innovation, because different people try different approaches. Oversight and risk management procedures can help minimize negative deviations while people experiment. And post-project debriefs allow teams to share how positive deviations came about so that others can build on their success.

This is a delicate balance, of course, but the outcome is that individuals will view work as more meaningful when they have some degree of autonomy in the process.

Ballistiq Digital

One company that does a great job of providing autonomy for its employees is Ballistiq Digital, a software development company headquartered in Montreal, Canada. Three partners founded Ballistiq in 2010: Leonard Teo and Kevin Strike in Montreal and Clarence Martens in Vancouver. The "mission" of Ballistiq is to "make a positive impact on people's lives through great software." As Teo states, "This guiding philosophy has helped us to create applications that are used and loved by millions of people worldwide."[29]

Ballistiq has succeeded with a distributed team of twenty-five employees. Although headquarters is in Montreal, the team works

---

29 Email from Leonard Teo to Richard J. Goossen dated January 26, 2017.

remotely from all across the country: Vancouver, Hamilton, Ottawa, Montreal, St John's, Quebec City, Nova Scotia, PEI. A Ballstiq subsidiary, ArtStation, has employees outside of Canada in Australia, Russia, and Ukraine. The company serves a global market. Of course, this type of distributed workforce is built on autonomy. This model was built into the founding of the company, as the founders were not from the same city. As the company expanded, it was born out of necessity. The competitive nature of the tech industry has made hiring in a single location extremely difficult, and it is hard to find good candidates all in the same location. There are amazing talents who for various reasons cannot live in large urban centers or "tech hubs" and are looking for good jobs that can be done remotely.

In addition to its consulting services, the company has developed a website called ArtStation, which is a "home for artists." As stated on its website, "ArtStation is the showcase platform for games, film, media & entertainment artists. It enables artists to showcase their portfolios in a slick way, discover & stay inspired, and connect with new opportunities."[30] For ArtStation, the company had to look offshore also out of necessity. It was impossible to hire senior technical people to work on a startup that wasn't funded. As Leonard Teo recalls,

> People thought we were crazy. There were so many other startups locally who were funded by venture capitalists and all the developers went to join these startups with the promise of stock options and getting rich (very few actually exited and all ended up working back at large companies). We had no choice but to look beyond Canada to get the best people.[31]

Teo went on to explain that

---

30 See www.artstation.com.
31 Email from Teo to Goossen.

The pricing works out similar. People think that offshoring to Russia is significantly cheaper—it's not, and we don't get any tax credits so it all works out to be on par. It's just driven purely by necessity—it's almost impossible to find senior software developers to work on your dinky little startup locally and all these local "A" players are being courted by the large tech companies and venture funded startups that you just can't compete.[32]

Why are autonomy and a distributed work force a viable approach? The answer is "lifestyle." As Teo explains:

Why work in the rat race? Why commute three hours a day to work in an office where you are staring at a screen and chatting on Slack, when there's technology now for video conferencing so that you don't have to be in the same office?[33]

From a practical standpoint, for some functions it is necessary to be in one spot. For example, Ballistiq has discovered that design/creativity tends to flow better in the same office. In those situations, they organize for people to fly in, do the deep dive for a couple of days, then go back again to work remotely. Having an HQ as a central anchor point is still important. As Teo explains, "We have an HQ in Montreal that we invest into for this reason. Our clients, and our partners, etc. all come into the office for meetings. All staff know that our HQ in Montreal is 'home base.'"[34] The advantages to this type of arrangement are twofold: Ballistiq can hire really great people and not be constrained by geography; and people are

---

32 Email from Teo to Goossen.
33 Email from Teo to Goossen.
34 Email from Teo to Goossen.

happier in their jobs. A further important advantage, Teo explains, is "We don't have to wear pants to go to work."[35]

Cofounder Kevin Strike noted that the distributed model was adopted

> Primarily so that we could focus on hiring great talent without being restricted to one specific geographic location. The tools available today diminish the need for being physically close. None of our customers are in the same geographic location as we are, so extending that to our team is a natural fit. Being a remote company does not benefit from some of the advantages that come naturally when everyone is in the same physical office. Daily group video conferences, heavy use of instant messaging and video chats, and semi-annual summit meetings at HQ are some of the habits we've implemented to develop a close team spirit.[36]

Strike points out the advantages: significant cost savings; significant productivity increases; the ability to attract talent worldwide; and the ability to attract talent that prefers working from home.[37] Strike notes that employees like this approach: "they love the independence, flexible work schedule, eliminate commute time, and they can spend more time in the home that they spend a significant amount of their income on."[38]

Clarence Martens explains the many benefits of autonomy from his own experience.[39] First, there is "a chance to interact with your family during the day." Second, he can "run a quick errand." Third, he can "go for a walk in his neighborhood, and see what is

---

35 Email from Teo to Goossen.
36 Email from Kevin Strike to Richard J. Goossen dated January 30, 2017.
37 Email from Strike to Goossen.
38 Email from Strike to Goossen.
39 Email from Clarence Martens to Richard J. Goossen dated January 30, 2017.

happening." Fourth, he has the "ability to handle more than one conversation at a time (e.g., chatting with two staff members at once, harder to do in person)." Fifth, he can "work with a wider range of people, potentially across the globe." Sixth, he has "flexible work schedules: besides mandated hours for meetings and customers, one can arrange a work day that maximizes your alertness and enthusiasm (maybe I am at my best in the morning, others would prefer night)." With autonomy comes responsibility. Employees need to be entrusted with getting the job done. As Martens muses,

> I'm also a bit mystified at the idea that a boss has to be physically present to watch the staff and make sure they are getting the work done. Surely one wants to hire employees that can be trusted, and there's better ways to determine work is being accomplished.[40]

11. SERVING

Another component of service leadership is the nature of the relationship between the employer and the employees. The more the organizational culture is one of concern for employees, the more engaged the employees are, the more committed they will be to the organization, and the more meaningful they will find the environment. This care for employees can be manifested in various ways. This is more of a challenge for larger organizations. In a smaller organization, the founder/owner can through force of personality make the personal connection with employees. In a larger organization, it needs to be embedded in the organizational culture.

We now look at several examples of companies whose leaders have led the way in caring for employees.

---

40 Email from Martens to Goossen.

Popeyes Louisiana Kitchen

Cheryl Bachelder is CEO of Popeyes Louisiana Kitchen based in Atlanta, GA, USA. Her focus is on running a company on the principles of servant leadership as a path to superior performance. As CEO since 2007, Cheryl has transformed Popeyes, a public company where she has created a workplace that inspires both service to one another and achievement of top-tier results. Her leadership has led to a 50 percent increase in market share, increased restaurant sales and profits, as well as a remarkable growth in the value of Popeyes' stock. Cheryl is known for reinvigorating great brands and inspiring leaders to reach their full potential—and the business outcomes are exceptional. She has embraced entrepreneurial concepts such as being an innovator in her industry and by empowering her fast-growing network of franchisees. She has more than thirty-five years of leadership experience in companies such as Procter & Gamble, the Gillette Company, and RJR Nabisco. Cheryl's book *Dare To Serve* has received praise from Stephen Covey, Ken Blanchard, and many other management experts.

At the time of Cheryl's appointment to the role of CEO in 2007, Popeyes' guest visits had been declining for years, and restaurant sales and profit trends were negative. The company stock price had dropped from $34 in 2002 to $13. The brand was stagnant, and relations between the company and its franchise owners were strained. Ms. Bachelder and her team created a workplace where people were treated with respect and dignity, yet challenged to perform at the highest level. Silos and self were set aside in favor of collaboration and team play. And the results were measured with rigor and discipline.

By 2014, average restaurant sales were up 25 percent, and profits were up 40 percent. Popeyes' market share had grown from 14 percent to 21 percent, and the stock price was over $40. In 2012, Ms. Bachelder was recognized as Leader of the Year by the Women's Foodservice Forum and received the highest industry award, the Silver Plate, for the quick service restaurant sector, presented by the International Food Manufacturers Association. She was also recognized as a 2012 Nation's Restaurant News' Golden Chain Award recipient.

Cheryl Bachelder has clearly achieved impressive results, all of which are grounded in her application of servant leadership and caring for her employees. She has established an organizational culture that reflects this approach.

ServiceMaster

We met William C. Pollard, former CEO and Board Chairman of ServiceMaster, in chapters 1 and 7. Bill's faith was imbedded in the ethos of ServiceMaster. The ServiceMaster objectives were simply stated: "To Honor God in All We Do; To Help People Develop; To Pursue Excellence; and To Grow Profitably" (Pollard, p. 95). He noted in his book *The Tides of Life*, "My prayer has been, and continues to be, that I will run the race of life in such a way that when it is over, my barns will be empty and my investments in sharing and serving will be completed" (p. 80). Bill has lived out his calling in the marketplace. Bill explained that

> One of the best ways I found to respond to God's call to the marketplace and to lead in the development of the firm as a moral community was to seek to serve as I led—to reflect the principles that Jesus taught His disciples as He washed their feet, including that fact that no leader is greater than those being led. As I sought to serve, the truth of what I said could be measured by what I did (p. 103).

OCK

Another example of someone who cares for his employees is Datuk Edward Ong.[41] Edward Ong is an accomplished builder and property

---

41 "Datuk" is an honorary title like "Sir."

developer. By the age of 40, Datuk Edward through his OCK Group in Singapore had completed numerous highly acclaimed projects including the Singapore General Hospital, the Apollo and Adelphi Hotels, Regency Park Condominium, and civil engineering works in three Mass Rapid Transit (MRT) stations. The group operations also covered projects and assignments in Malaysia, Burma, and the Commonwealth of the Northern Mariana Island—Saipan and Guam.

He began his journey of faith at age forty. Although he had achieved success in the eyes of the world up to that point, he began to realize that success without purpose is life without meaning. In the mid-90s, he started the Sutera Harbour Resort project, which is designed as a world-class resort in the heart of Kota Kinabalu, Sabah, Malaysia, on 384 acres of prime seafront reclaimed land. The resort offers two five-star hotels, a twenty-seven-hole championship golf course, a 104-berth marina, and extensive facilities at Sutera Harbour Marina, Golf & Country Club. The total project cost was USD 450 million. The resort employs 1,800 staff and is the second largest employer in the state. The journey to complete this project had been fraught with challenges and obstacles, physical, mental, political, and financial, that seemed insurmountable from a human's point of view, but with the Lord all things are possible. He had worked in His amazing way to ensure the completion of the project for His glory.

Currently, Datuk Edward is leaving his comfort zone on a new journey to develop a USD 300 million integrated resort in Dili, Timor-Leste, complete with a 492-room hotel, golf course, hillside villas, a business park, and condominiums. The resort is expected to employ at least 1,200 staff at completion. This will also be a project notable not so much for its financial achievement, but for giving back to society, to provide training to the locals and, with the skills learned, to give them a chance of a better life for them and their families.

Far East Organization

Philip Ng is CEO, Far East Organization (FEO), Singapore. FEO is the largest private property developer in Singapore. Since its establishment in 1960, FEO has been contributing to the transformation of Singapore's urban landscape with over 770 developments in the residential, hospitality, retail, commercial, and industrial sectors, FEO's listed entities comprise Far East Orchard Limited, Yeo Hiap Seng Limited, and Far East Hospitality Trust. Launched in 2012, Far East Hospitality Trust is the first and only Singapore-focused hotel and serviced residence hospitality trust listed on the Singapore Exchange Securities Trading Limited (SGX-ST). It is also Singapore's largest diversified hospitality portfolio by asset value. FEO has a network of regional offices with presence in key cities in China, Indonesia, and Australia. FEO's hospitality and property group, Far East Orchard, has established joint ventures in the hospitality business with The Straits Trading Company and Toga Group, Australia, with a global portfolio of close to 90 properties and more than 13,000 rooms across seven countries. FEO is the only developer in the world to be bestowed ten FIABCI Prix d'Excellence Awards, underscoring its unique achievements in the international real estate arena.

FEO takes a unique approach to setting up a corporate culture.[42] The vision is to "Inspire Better Lives." Philip Ng's personal faith is reflected in the company's mission. The mission: "We are a Christian Enterprise, which develops real estate and operates businesses by serving with grace and love, integrity and honesty."[43] The core values are "BUILD," which stands for B—Business with Grace; U—Unity; I—Integrity; L—Love; and D—Diligence. FEO has a clear enterprise statement:

> Far East Organization is a Christian enterprise. We seek to be
> a community of love and a workplace of grace that welcomes

---

42 http://www.fareast.com.sg/en/about-us/core-values.
43 FEO website.

Christians and non-Christians alike to work joyfully together. As we join hands to build a garden of enterprise that endures (to honor the vision of our late founder, Mr Ng Teng Fong), we want to do good business and to do good in business.[44]

This fits in with one of the service leadership factors we discussed in earlier chapters that relate to respecting faith, even when people have a different faith from one's own.

FEO further elaborates:

As a Christian enterprise, we embrace the eternal truths of God's Word. We apply these truths to our business as these are words of life and business is, after all, a part of life itself. Thus, we operate our business on the solid foundation of our values and our rock that is Jesus Christ. Our core values are Business with Grace, Unity, Integrity, Love, Diligence and we practice these values alongside the teachings of Jesus. Our Christian identity is integral to the brand of Far East Organization. . . . Our focus is on fulfilment, governed by the principles of Stewardship and Grace. Fulfilment entails fulfilling our mission, our objectives and our lives in the Way of Jesus Christ.

Philip Ng shares his thoughts on material wealth, anxieties, and God's grace:

I am in business and business is about money. But money and possessions can possess us. How then do I serve God as a businessperson? The way to do this is to realize that I am a steward; the Lord has entrusted money to me to be managed responsibly. At the end of the day, we take nothing with us. I saw this when my father passed away (Ng, 2015).

---

44 Philip Ng, "The Journey of a Christian Enterprise," Global Business Network Asian Marketplace Conference, July 14, 2016, Singapore.

Philip Ng explained:

> My life has changed because of the Lord. I do morning
> devotions, I pray because there is much I do not understand.
> I pray for discernment, for guidance. God makes sense of all
> situations. He made sense of what I went through with my
> father just before he passed away. My father was not a pagan
> worshipper but he did not have time for God; he was too
> busy running his business. He did not object when he knew
> that I had come to Christ. In fact, he always talked to me
> about meeting his Maker one day (ibid.).

Philip Ng also noted,

> I tell my people in the organization that when we do busi-
> ness, we want to do good business and to do good in busi-
> ness. That is my call to them. But we welcome and certainly
> include those from other faiths. We hope that our message of
> love can truly find a place in their hearts (ibid.).

Minutrade, Brazil

Another example of caring for employees comes from Eduard Jacob,
MinuTrade, São Paolo, Brazil. Eduard Jacob explains that in 1998,
he started his first entrepreneurial venture at the age of 29. The name
of the company was "Nuts network," and the product was called
"Divertix." His idea was to create a global entertainment access platform based on the venue's access infrastructure. A person could buy
a "ticket" through the phone or via the Internet using a contactless
card that would be recognized at the venue access system, making a
physical ticket unnecessary.

Jacob explains how the company started: "I'd like to sketch out
some of the context in which the MinuTrade idea and operation

were conceived because it throws some light on the commercial and social goals we're trying to achieve."[45] He explains that

> There are approximately 180 million cell phone plans in Brazil. The vast majority of them (around 83%) are linked to pre-paid plans. And there are only four main carriers (Vivo, Claro, Tim and Oi). . . . The banks in Brazil have issued 150 million credit cards, most of them linked to programs that give rewards to their users in proportion to how much they spend on their card. The system can be compared to "air miles" reward programs. The focus is on those social groups that tend to spend the most. . . . An idea occurred to us that became our mission: to offer a micro reward platform that would allow those on low incomes to participate in the rewards programs of the banks. . . . To make this happen, we decided to create a prize that could be exchanged for a small number of points ("miles") from the reward programs. It would allow people with limited spending power to exchange their few points for a useful prize. . . . The added value of the prize would need to be obvious to those at the bottom of the economic pyramid, who tend to use pay-as-you-go, rather than contract, schemes. For many of them, the cost of cell phone calls is an important item in their monthly expenses because effective communication is often a top priority in gaining or sustaining employment opportunities.

Jacob created the MinuTrade brand, which is a combination of the words "minute" and "trade." His concept was to facilitate the

---

45 This and all subsequent Jacob quotes are from the Peter S. Heslam interview with Eduardo Jacob, July 6, 2010, in Richard J. Goossen, ed., *Entrepreneurial Leaders: Reflections on Faith at Work* (Vol. 5), Langley, BC: Trinity Western University, 2010, pp 79–92.

trading of rewards points for minutes of cell phone conversation. Jacob explains that

> Because the prize is of low cost, the logistic cost would also need to be kept as low as possible. Digital delivery provided the means to achieve this. It allows us to maximize the volume of transactions. Because we target a large percentage of the population, we generate millions of small transactions.
> [...]
> I have also used MinuTrade's platform to develop projects in partnership with governmental agencies. These programs forge a new communication channel between government programs and people on low incomes. The overall aim is to increase social inclusion by increasing digital inclusion.
> [...]
> MinuTrade is a business to business (B to B) company. MinuTrade is the first micro rewards platform in Brazil. The company distributes cell phone air-time (minutes of conversation) from different carriers through promotion, incentive programs or rewards programs of our clients.

Jacob explains his motivation:

> With respect to MinuTrade, we have a unique vision. We achieve commercial success by combining technological innovation with social goals. It's what gets us out of bed every morning. I pray at the office thanking God and asking for direction. I invite our employees to pray with me on a weekly basis and some of them take up this invitation. I also pray with my partners. My door is always open and I'm very willing for people to share with me any personal problems and to pray with them. I openly share my faith in my company. I do this through praying in my office. My Bible is open all the time on my desk. People come to see me in my office with problems

and I offer to pray for them, whether or not they are Christian. People have come to faith this way. I invite them to join those of us who regularly meet to pray in the company and some of them accept this invitation and come along.

Polaris

Polaris is a major financial technology company that works in the IT space as a global outsourcing and system integrator. With widely accepted products, legacy modernization, and IT services, it is a publicly traded major company on the Bombay Stock Exchange. It specializes in banking, asset management, and insurance and has a strong reputation for innovation and intelligent design.

The company was founded in 1993 as one of the first vendors of Citi Group when it started doing business in India. Later renamed Orbitech, it was then merged with Polaris Ltd., in 2003. Headquartered in the southern region of India, in Chennai, Tamil Nadu, the company has offices throughout India and around the world. With a large Indian employee base, the company has become acclaimed for its design thinking and its design center that allows its corporate clients to experience the future at first hand.

The founder of Polaris is Arun Jain, who has remained as its seminal leader throughout its upward trajectory and phenomenal growth. Jain is himself a strict Jainist, and that background colors the company's values and orientation. Based in the Indian Jainist tradition, yet cutting edge in terms of technology prowess, the company has built up a number of exemplar service-oriented practices and over time institutionalized them. The Jainist dimension of leadership can be seen in three specific areas as articulated by Arun Jain, in interviews with him and his senior team. These areas are: corporate social responsibility (CSR), Ullas Trust, and Sampada.

In Polaris, CSR, or corporate citizenship, is not just an involvement in charitable or philanthropic activities due to business responsibility, but the organization's conscious decision to support social, economic, and ethical responsibilities. CSR practice is embedded in the entire organizational culture and is part of its way to give back to the society where they live and owe its growth.

Ullas Trust (a Polaris initiative) was started in 1997 by the Polaris employees themselves, with an aim to integrate Polaris within a larger community and enable them to enjoy working with young minds across India. The primary motive of Ullas was to recognize academic excellence in students from the economically challenged sections of Indian society and encourage a "Can Do" spirit toward chasing their dreams and aspirations. Very early in its evolution, Ullas decided to focus its energies on students during the most vulnerable stage in their journey—adolescence. And the program has brought tens of hundreds of needy but very bright students up from poverty.

Sampada was launched by Laser Soft Info systems, a group company of Polaris. The initiative involves recruiting people with disabilities or differently abled people to work across different levels in the organization. The program has won awards for its social value in Indian society and from the government.

The tradition of Jainism and its strong values impacts on the way the Chairman, CEO, and the company senior leaders approach the business and is demonstrated in these unique and powerful service-oriented ways.

12. LISTENING AND RESPECT

One important aspect of service leadership is the notion of respecting people, giving them face, and treating them with dignity. In Western society, these concepts are increasingly less practiced in general interaction, so it is rare to find a company that practices respectful interaction. Do people appreciate it? Absolutely. There are not many people who would claim that they don't mind being disrespected. And, of course, this dynamic exists up and down the organizational chart. When people feel they have been disrespected, they will exact retribution in both small and large ways. This can be as simple as the janitor who doesn't open the office door in off-hours because the executive doesn't have prior authorization or the office servers intentionally banging dishes and cutlery, in a sense proclaiming that they matter, too! The notion of respecting employees can take shape in various ways.

Amortegui (2014) notes:

> If you consider yourself part of the 70% of disengaged employees in America, what could a boost of meaning at work do for you? Organizational consultant David Cooperrider subscribes to the notion that "what we appreciate, appreciates." If we begin to appreciate the meaning that infiltrates our daily workplaces, then we will grow our capacity to seek it, and seize it. This, in turn, will increase the value of meaningfulness in our work and ensure that it gains the esteemed position it so desperately deserves: a position alongside happiness.

We will look at some companies that understand the importance of respect and appreciation.

Phantom Screens

Esther de Wolde of Phantom Screens, referenced earlier, says, "speak the truth with each other. And it's not only what you say, but it's what you don't say. We feel that everyone should be respected equally and served because each person is created in the image of God." She understands the important role of respecting all members of the team. Of course, this notion of respecting employees crosses faith lines. De Wolde explains:

> We don't expect all our staff to be Christians, in fact, I look to hire more non-Christians to have hopefully a positive

effect on their lives, but we just explain where we are coming from so they understand. It's pretty clear where our strength comes from as owners.

Martinrea

Rob Wildeboer of Martinrea says:

> As a leader, I am, and I feel, personally responsible, along with the senior members of our team, for the wellbeing and welfare of our people. The key to our success as leaders, to my success as a leader, is whether our company is taking care of our people and their future. I am an ambassador for what we do, to our people, to our customers, to our stakeholders, and to the governments of the places in which we do business.

He understands well the importance of treating people well. He further notes that

> In order to perform our mission and fulfill our vision, we have also developed, in conjunction with our people at the corporate level, in the groups and in the plants, the principles that will guide how we do business. We believe our success will ultimately be based on the application and execution of our guiding principles, applied with integrity, in all that we do.

Silulo Ulutho Technologies

Luvuyo Rani is the founder of Silulo Ulutho Technologies, an all-in-one provider of information technology (IT)-related products and services headquartered in Khayelitsha township in Cape Town, South Africa. This includes computer training skills, business services, website development, computer and accessory retail sales, and repair and maintenance services. Targeting young and middle-aged township residents of the Western Cape, Silulo serves a largely untapped niche market due to a lack of IT access in these areas. Silulo has built an extended network of supporters and local organizations throughout the communities in which it is involved. This network has played a powerful role in the development of the business and is key to the company's overall marketing strategy.

Rani explains that

The vision and drive of Silulo stems from three basic concepts: technology, knowledge and empowerment. Technology enables communication and collaboration across social and cultural barriers. Knowledge comes from the impulse to learn and to exceed limitations. Empowerment is about enabling people to create opportunity for themselves and allowing them to surpass expectations and optimize their potential. The partners and employees of Silulo are dedicated to inspiring people to take their futures into their own hands. We want to help people uplift themselves and their communities through the power of knowledge and technology.[46]

Our business is situated within the township of Khayelitsha. Many residents in the townships of South Africa still do not have access to the digital world. Two thirds of Khayelitsha residents aged 15–65 are either unemployed or not economically active. Unskilled people have little chance of finding employment. Training can help these people to improve their chances of finding employment. Or, better still, to start their own small businesses, which not

---

46 This and subsequent Rani quotations are taken from the Peter S. Heslam interview with Luvuyo Rani in Richard J. Goossen, ed. *Entrepreneurial Leaders: Reflections on Faith at Work* (Vol. 5), Langley, BC: Trinity Western University, 2010, pp 169–179.

only enables them to feed themselves and their families but provides employment opportunities for others.

The cost of unemployment is substantial. It is costly not only in terms of health and education schemes but also in terms of crime levels, population growth, and the impairment of natural resources. Acquiring computer skills that result in employment contributes to the dignity and self-sufficiency of individuals. And it also boosts, rather than drains, government resources through the various taxes, rates and levies that are imposed on business.

We believe it is our duty to help fix this problem. To do so in a sustainable way, we realized that we needed to partner with big companies. Once we set up a business center (including an Internet café) in a township, it becomes a hub of the community, facilitating communication and business-related activities in an area where there is little access to local service provision. Silulo's activities and expansion plan create the potential for clients to up-skill themselves and increase their chances of accessing employment, including the opportunity for some of them to access employment directly from Silulo as an expanding local business.

In terms of job creation, a Silulo business center (including an Internet café) employs a staff of five and a Silulo training center requires three trainers. Silulo's current staff complement is nineteen and seven of those have been recruited from Silulo's training program. With each of our new branches we expect three to five new jobs to be created that are appropriate for our training program trainees.

Through our training, we stimulate further employment within the townships. We have trained approximately 1,500 students and we understand that approximately 60% of them have found employment. Through expansion we aim to train more than a thousand students a year. Maintaining our current student employment rates, approximately 1,000 students per year will have greatly increased their chances of securing employment.

As far as our training program content is concerned, we don't just train our students in computer skills. We also train them in communication skills and work readiness programs to prepare them for job interviews. We deliver these services in partnership with other companies such as TeleTech and Impumelelo Staffing Solutions (ISS). Our work readiness program with ISS equips students with the necessary skills to source employment. But ISS also looks out for opportunities that can benefit our students after completing the course, such as a job or placement in that company.

We are helping individuals to have access to the digital world and we're helping to empower them through the establishment of business centers and training centers. But we also support groups—local schools, churches, local businesses and various types of organizations—with their information and communication technology needs.

How does Rani treat people?

I always try to treat people the same, whether they are Christian or not. With another Christian you can, of course, share more easily where you're coming from. But most people of good will operate within the same general principles and most of these principles are based on Christian values. Because of the pervasiveness of Christianity in our environment [in South Africa], most people understand the core of the gospel and that Christ died for them, even if they don't go to church.

Costco

An excellent example of how to treat people well comes from Richard Galanti, Executive Vice President and Chief Financial Officer of Costco Wholesale Corporation, whom we met in Chapter 7. He explains the foundation of how to treat stakeholders and employees:

> I think the foundation is when Jim [Sinegal] and Jeff [Brotman] [the cofounders], really Jim, wrote the basic five tenets of how we operate the business. This wasn't done after Enron and Tyco and all the scandals; this was done twenty-six years ago. The five tenets, in this order, are: obey the law; take care of your customers; take care of your employees; be tough but fair with your vendors; and, if you accomplish those things, then you will take care of your shareholders.[47]
>
> Shareholders think that's fine as long as you show good earnings and you are growing nicely. During the 1990s, for example, earnings were up 20–25 percent a year compounded, our stock was selling at more than 30x earnings, when our peers were selling at 15–18x earnings, and we could do no wrong. It's great that we pay our hourly employees very well. We give them great health benefits, which by US standards is a very rich plan and a very low cost to the employee. And that's all great as long as our earnings are growing. In the early 2000s, as we were ramping up expansion in the markets and we stubbed our toe a couple of times, meaning that earnings were about flat for a couple of years, then all of a sudden, "Why are you paying your people so well? Why are you so crazy on lowering prices all the time, in terms of low markups?" We are in it for the long term. Wall Street sometimes views the long term differently.

47 This and subsequent Galanti quotations are from the Richard J. Goossen interview with Richard Galaniti, CFO, Costco, Issaquah, WA, USA, January 25, 2010.

Some on Wall Street say "the problem with Costco is that long term is twenty-forty, not ten, years from now". And, of course, Jim's view was the problem with Wall Street is that "long term" is next Tuesday. Somewhere in the middle is probably the right answer.

A very basic statement such as "Obey the Law" can be everything from adhering to foreign corrupt trade practices laws to not skimping on how much landscaping is required in an asphalt parking lot. We try to exceed expectations at every juncture. On pricing we don't mark things below cost unless we have made a mistake. We don't have loss leaders nor do we mark up goods more than 15%. Our view is that no matter how smart or good we are, and no matter how great the buyer thinks he or she is in getting good value . . . if you don't limit your mark-ups, then one day you find others are pricing as low as you. And all of a sudden you're not so special.

Another aspect is our open door policy. A lot of companies say that you can always speak to people at the highest level, but it is not so in practice. I've sat in Jim's office and the phone rings and it's an hourly employee that is suspended, pending termination, for something he or she did at a warehouse in Texas. Jim will take his or her name and number down. Needless to say nine out of ten times he doesn't reverse the decision but he makes sure they've been treated fairly. And you know what you find out by doing that? You find out sometimes we're not always perfect out there. Perhaps a certain manager shows favoritism. You dig a little deeper and you find out there are issues. These might not be terminable issues with the manager, but there may be things that you need to address in order to be fair with everybody.

Here at our central headquarters office [in Issaquah, WA] we have almost 3,000 employees. We have three office buildings that are connected. We have about 1,800 car parking spaces. Not all of them are assigned. But the roughly 100 under each building are the best ones. They are not hot in the summer and they are not wet and cold in the winter and you don't have to walk 200 yards out to your car. These parking spots are not assigned based on position, but on tenure. So I have one either way because I've been here for 26 years. But next to me is an hourly accounts payable clerk. That was done by Jim years ago, not because it will be perceived as fair but because it's the right thing to do. So we try to "walk the walk" of being fair. We try to be honest with our customers, good to our employees, and tough but fair with our vendors.

Having an open door policy doesn't mean that any employee can just jump from their immediate manager to talk to the President. But if they go through the channels, they talk to their supervisor, they talk to the manager, they talk to the regional VP, and they really feel they are not being treated fairly, they have every right to talk to Jim.

We take this same approach with customers. One example is when we changed our returns policy on electronics from infinity to 90 days. With the obsolescence of products, we were getting returns every 90–100 days. Customers would simply return their old iPod and buy the new one because it was $10 cheaper, it had four times the memory and it had a screen. We were losing, literally, $200 million a year on salvage costs of electronics. So we changed this policy. The best policy in the market, other than Costco, is 30 days and it's only 100 cents on the dollar if you don't open the item. There is a restocking charge if you even open the box. At Costco our policy was: you don't need a receipt, you don't need a box, just bring it back. We had people bring back their old TV set every three or so years to buy a new one. They would end up walking out with a new TV that was ten times better and $400 in cash.

We had to stop that. Needless to say, when we changed the policy we received 50 or 100 irate letters and emails generally saying that, "You are punishing everybody for the few that abuse the privilege." One lady wrote a letter saying one of the biggest reasons she shopped at Costco for 20 years was the free annual TV upgrade. She was being honest. You know what? We took all those letters and emails and we gave them to 10 senior executives to call these people. Virtually every one of those individuals that was honestly upset thanked us and couldn't believe that we were actually calling. But more importantly, that's how we run our business.

You can't run a retail business from behind a desk; you have to be out in the warehouses. Every business is different. If you are involved in genetic engineering, you need to be behind your Petri dishes. But in retail you have to be seeing what your own company is doing, seeing what your competition is doing, seeing what is at trade shows. Jim walks the floor of our stores with a manager and the assistant managers and, he's asking them questions, "When did we go up on Tide? What does the competition sell this for?" The manager should be running the store like it's his or her own business. This gives you a little flavor of staying honest to those core values that we started with.

What are the sustainable competitive advantages of Costco?

I think our competitive advantage starts with the fact that we treat our people well. I will use US$ numbers; but it's comparable in any of the eight countries where we operate. Our goal is always to hire the best people. We are able to do that by paying them a higher wage, getting them to the top of the scale faster over a certain number of hours, providing them with high quality affordable benefits, promoting from within, and hopefully providing everybody with opportunities who want opportunities. If you look at the union supermarkets, all big successful big box retailers, the average hourly wage is $12.50 to $14.50 an hour. At Costco in the US it's a little over $19. I can probably make the case that $18 is more profitable and that you are not going to reduce efficiency very much, if any; maybe at $16.50 you start. But we've started with the premise, what is the right thing to do?

I am biased, but our approach helps us get the best employees. By contrast, when you go into different retailers, particularly little neighborhood retailers, you do not see "engaged" employees. It is different at Costco. Our people are engaged. We're going to make mistakes out there; but by and large they care about the company and they like working for us. It's nice to work for a company where both your customers and your employees like you and trust you. We've done everything possible forever to make them trust us. I sometimes joke with Jim, "You know I don't mind walking over the hot coals barefooted but do I have to hit myself with the chain at the same time?" We take everything to the extreme, in terms of about how we can be a sustainable, tough competitor and to have great employees, too.

Marriott

Marriott was founded in 1927 by J.W Marriott, a faithful Mormon from Utah, as a root beer stand in Washington, DC. It started selling hot food and became Hot Shoppes—a family restaurant chain. They operated contracts for food service and in 1957 shifted into the hotel business with the opening of the world's first motor hotel. By 1977, revenue had grown to $1 billion a year. By 2015, Marriott International and its affiliates managed well over three thousand hotels and other properties worldwide, divided into 18 different brands in a broad range of market segments, including luxury hotels and resorts, full service hotels, limited service hotels, extended stay lodging, and timeshares. With over 600,000 hotel rooms in seventy-three countries, it enjoys one of the largest market shares in its industry.

At the heart of the Marriott image is an attitude toward its workers. This is what makes Marriott Marriott. According to Bill Marriott, the son of the founder, "If the employees are well taken care of, they'll take care of the customer and the customer will come back." That is the core value at Marriott.

The company is consistently on the list of top one hundred companies to work at, one of only two hotel companies on that coveted list. Mormonism has an unmistakable presence at Marriott. The family still owns roughly 25 percent of the company, and members of the family play an important role on the board or as executives.

The *Book of Mormon* is placed in every room, but few explicit Mormon fingerprints are to be found. The atmosphere is one of serving and leadership. Notably, the company always tries to take the high road in its work and negotiations: no dishonesty and no hard tactics. Marriott is a service company in a service hospitality industry that is colored by its belief systems and its fair treatment of its people.

Kraft

Kraft is a manufacturing giant present in over 150 countries and in 99 percent of US households. The company boasts a profoundly humanistic version of servant leadership. The CEO, Irene Rosenfeld, has called servant leadership central to the company's management framework, as it inspires the company to serve its workers and the communities in which it operates. The view is that this in turn creates greater value for the company. From sustainability programs to new product development and from philanthropic initiatives to marketing, servant leadership shapes the practices within this iconic company and the world's second largest food company.

While the CEO is not alone in her advocacy of the framework of servant leadership, Rosenfeld strongly emphasizes the overall value of servant leadership in the management at Kraft. She says, "the people that work with me understand . . . I am there to help them, not for them to help me."

To the senior staff at Kraft, servant leadership is about "encouraging employees to strive for in new and inspiring ways both personally and professionally." Servant leadership is cited as a concept that sees employees' needs as ends in themselves.

This view of leading is rooted in the humanistic conviction that a company should enhance its employees and the society in which it operates. This form of humanism expresses a commitment to advance the well-being of others and contribute positively to society, morally and materially.

At Kraft, this has meant taking values seriously and developing morality and calling in the ranks. Kraft's CSR activities develop a robust values-based story about the company that also appeals to its customers.

The origins of servant leadership at Kraft go back to the AT&T executive Robert Greenleaf who first coined the term in an effort to elicit management styles that were both effective and transformative for society. For Greenleaf, this begins with the natural desire to serve. Helping others come first. To quote Greenleaf, "The goal of servant leadership is directly or indirectly to improve the autonomy of others—it moves from people-using to people-building."

The test for Greenleaf and at Kraft is observable. It is always: "Do those served grow as persons? Do they, while being served, become healthier, wiser, freer, more autonomous, more likely themselves to become servants?"

Rosenfeld in her tenure at Kraft took on a mantle of a visibly humanistic outlook, seeking to make a difference in two areas. Kraft came to believe that its employees should become better people as a result of having worked at Kraft and that society should also be better as a result of Kraft having done business with it. Two core values are trust and ownership: it values trust among its employees and within the communities where it has consumers; and it values accountability to the constituents it affects.

This sense of service in leadership is diligently practiced at Kraft and is grounded in a desire to serve and fulfill its aims. As Greenleaf himself urged, "servant leadership should improve those being served." That is the ambition at Kraft, even as it has experienced mergers, acquisitions, and a division of the company.

More recently, it has been embodied in its various health and wellness initiatives and in its environmental efficiency. Water, waste, and energy all represent key areas of increased sustainability for Kraft globally. Philanthropically, Kraft has a record that supports its humanistic goal of improving others' lives through corporate operations. Kraft has invested in large-scale hunger elimination and poverty reduction programs following its servant mentality and commitment.

Timberland

The outdoor apparel company was started in the 1950s when its founder, Nathan Swartz, purchased a Boston shoe company. Moving to New Hampshire, it developed waterproof boots under the name Timberland. The company grew into an international designer and marketer, distributing footwear, apparel, and various accessories for men and women. The company was eventually sold to the conglomerate VF but remains a division in the larger entity.

Jeff Swartz's leadership is what made the brand and culture. His family stewarded the company for generations. They focused in large part on instilling a culture of service among those who work at the company. In Swartz's own words in an interview a decade ago:

I honestly get deep joy watching my colleagues invest some of their Path of Service volunteer hours to compost and mulch and sow and reap organic produce, which is sold in our headquarters, with the proceeds going to feed the working poor here.

Timberland revolves around community service. Sustainability is a hallmark of the leadership philosophy of Timberland: sustainability within its business environment, with regards to both the natural world and the communities in which it operates.

Service at Timberland has many dimensions, as witnessed in Swartz's testimony. Excellence as an employer is foremost, and it comes from this aspect of community building. It attracts the best talent and articulates a code of conduct that memorializes progressive and humane leadership in employment.

Timberland's efforts in a proactive and responsible stewardship over the environment are summarized in what the company calls "Earthkeeping." The company was an early and ardent proponent of CSR. As a pioneer in the field before it became popular, the company pushed ecofriendly policies in the early 1990s. The company became and remains a model for many other companies.

CONCLUSION

Two decades ago, the respected business author Jim Collins and academic Jerry Porras published a book about the organizational underpinnings of economic life that shouted out against the ethic of impermanence. Titled *Built To Last*, it described a model and a number of companies that fit that model and that were indeed going to last because of the way they were organized and the values they incorporated from the beginning.

Built to Last certainly hit a chord with readers and business leaders. It has had more than seventy printings worldwide, been translated into seventeen languages, and enjoyed fifty-five months on the *Business Week* bestseller lists. What it suggested was something unexpected yet also commonsensical.

According to Collins, the book did so well because "people were beginning to ask themselves, 'is nothing sacred? Is nothing timeless? Is nothing sustainable?'" and because it gave people a perspective "that they desperately craved." It said, "Yes, there are some timeless fundamentals. They apply today, and we need them now more than ever." And it "affirmed that the essence of [business] greatness does not lie in cost cutting, restructuring, or the pure profit motive." Instead, "it lies in people's dedication to building companies around a sense of purpose—around core values that infuse work with the kind of meaning that goes beyond just making money." Interestingly, the subtitle of the book is "successful habits of visionary companies." The companies found success because they habituated meaning and infused it into their ideologies.

The book endures because it is not about one-off charismatic leaders, or visionary product concepts, or some visionary insights into the market(s), near or far. It is not about having the all-too-familiar corporate vision statement, and most decidedly not about putting it on laminated cards and sticking it to your refrigerator door, only to be forgotten or ignored.

The theme of lasting companies is far more important, deep, and enduring. It is about visionary companies themselves. It is their essence and their very DNA that make them who they are and allow them to have permanence, when and where so many others fail. Based on extensive empirical research at Stanford University's Graduate School of Business, the study looked at eighteen truly exceptional companies and directly compared them to their top competitors. The work asked a simple question: what makes a truly exceptional company different than other companies?

The framework that emerged was both coherent and practical. It could be applied as a master blueprint for building any organization that wanted to prosper for a long, long time.

And what was the key, overarching finding?

Lasting companies must have a devotion to a core ideology that helps their employees align with a deep commitment to the company. Only such engaged employees can find their own purpose in the larger purpose of the companies they choose (and who choose them). This calling is two-sided.

This concept of service to and by companies is at the core of what we have described in this treatment of what we have termed service leadership. It starts with a calling, which makes sense of larger reality and is shaped by a larger purpose. This gives meaning on numerous levels to people in their working lives, on the job and in their directed vocations. Service leadership, as considered in this book, takes many forms and is not uniformly the same. It is a process and not an exclusively personal attribute. We can and want to learn how to become service leaders. As human beings, we have a natural bent in that direction, no matter where we live, where we work, or what we do.

Companies and employees who together habituate to this practice are more likely to last, as Collins found. These employees are more likely to be happy and satisfied. They are more productive and engaged, and in the end, they are more fulfilled.

Companies would be well served to take heed and, in this twenty-first century, strive to become oriented and attuned to service leadership. The results will be powerful for everyone involved.

ENTREPRENEURIAL LEADERS
QUESTIONNAIRE

Name of Entrepreneur: _____

Company _____

Interviewers: (1)_____& (2)_____

Date of Interview: _____Location: _____

NOTE TO INTERVIEWEE

Thank you very much for your involvement. Your participation is greatly valued and appreciated. The objective of the interview is to accumulate your insights as a leader with those of others, and to produce research that will be of value and interest to entrepreneurs and business leaders.

For the purposes of this questionnaire, an "entrepreneur" is a person who pursues innovation, assembles resources, and undertakes and assesses risk for the purpose of making a profit. While entrepreneurship can and does occur in many types and sizes or organizations, the focus of this research project is primarily on individuals who have started a high-growth business or who have significantly transformed an existing business.

The other aspect of this questionnaire is to understand the impact of how being a normative leader impacts an individual's approach to entrepreneurship. Our intent is to identify individuals who actively practice their beliefs and who are striving to apply principles in their entrepreneurial pursuits.

Please contact me directly if you have any concerns, comments, or suggestions regarding this questionnaire or the interview:

SECTION A. BACKGROUND INFORMATION

This information is strictly private and confidential and is requested for data analysis that is not disclosed in relation to you personally and is not for publication.

Name: _____

Address: _____

_____

Off / Cell: _____   Res: _____

Fax: _____   Email: _____

Sex: Male _____   Female _____

Martial Status: Single _____   Married: ____Divorced ____Widowed ____

Number of Children: _____

Number of Years as Entrepreneur: _____[your "entrepreneurial career"]

Post-secondary education/training (as applicable, for each institution)

Description	Institution #1	Institution #2	Institution #3
Name of Institution			
Program			
Degree/ Certificate (e.g., Bachelor of Business Administration)			
Years Attended (e.g., 2000–2004)			

Place of Birth: _____   Date of Birth (dd/mth/yr): _____
Background: _____

I attend religious services this often on an annual basis (circle one):
 1—10
 11–20
 21–30
 31–40
 41–52

I read the sacred literature this often per month (circle one):
 1–5
 6–10
 11–15
 16–20
 21–25
 26–30

I pray this often per week (circle one):
 1–7
 8–14
 15–21

I am presently involved in "para-Church" organizations (list two at most):

Name of Organization: _____
Type of Involvement (circle one or more, as applicable):
 a. I provide financial support;
 b. I am actively involved in doing something;
 c. I go on short term missions trips;
 d. I am involved at a board level.

Name of Organization: _____

Type of Involvement (circle one or more, as applicable):

  a. I provide financial support;
  b. I am actively involved in doing something;
  c. I go on short term missions trips;
  d. I am involved at a board level.

SECTION B. COMPANY BACKGROUND

If the entrepreneur is retired, semiactive, or an investor, then the focus of Part II is on their most significant past business involvement. The below information is intended to provide context and chronology to the entrepreneur's comments.

List companies in chronological order, starting with the most recent:

Description	Company #1	Company #2
Dates of Involvement		
Title		
Name of Company		
Website		
Location(s)		
# of Employees		
Product/ Service		
Industry		
Revenue (range)		
Public / Private		
Description	**Company #3**	**Company #4**
Dates		
Title		
Name of Company		
Website		
Location(s)		

# of Employees		
Product/ Service		
Industry		
Revenue (range)		
Public / Private		

SECTION C. QUESTIONNAIRE CHART

State to what extent you agree with the below statements.
1 = Strongly Disagree; 5 = Average; and 10 = Strongly Agree:

#	Question	Rating (1–10)
1	The pastor of my church is interested in my business dealings.	
2	I feel my pastor understands what I do for a living.	
3	I feel that when the pastor speaks from the pulpit on business-related matters, he is accurate and insightful.	
4	Members within a congregation should do business together as a way of supporting one another if the opportunity arises.	
5	I have discovered my sense of meaning / direction / calling in business and have integrated it with my faith largely through my own efforts.	
6	I am involved in business because I believe that is God's plan for me and that the workplace is my mission field.	
7	I view my business primarily not as a ministry but as a place to make money so that this can then allow me to financially support worthwhile ministries.	
8	I generally feel more comfortable working with parachurch organizations rather than churches in order to utilize what I believe are my gifts as an entrepreneur.	

9	Pastors and churches should get involved in a business dispute between myself and another Christian in order to bring about reconciliation.	
10	Christians should have no qualms about suing non-Christians, if I believe they have violated the law.	
11	Christians should have no qualms about suing Christians, if I believe they have violated the law.	
12	I believe biblical principles provide guidance as to how I should conduct myself in a business context.	
13	A Christian in the workplace (even the owner or partner in a company) should be able to deliberately witness or share the gospel with coworkers.	
14	A Christian in the workplace should witness by his or her behavior and share the gospel only when another individual asks questions.	
15	Christians are forbidden by the Bible to enter into business partnerships with nonbelievers.	
16	Christians can enter into partnerships with non-Christians and can effectively witness on their own.	
17	Based on my business experience, the reputation of Christians in the workplace is that they are generally people of integrity.	
18	Based on my business experience, there is a clear difference between the actions of Christians and non-Christians in the workplace.	
19	I find meaning in my work because I believe God wants me to be doing what I am doing.	
20	I believe God blesses business people in proportion to the degree they follow a Christian approach to life.	

SECTION D. ORAL INTERVIEW QUESTIONS

I. General Entrepreneurship Questions

NOTE: *The comments in italics throughout the interview are for guidance and are not included in the final transcript.*

1. At what age did you start your first entrepreneurial venture, and what was it?
2. What originally motivated you to pursue entrepreneurship, and what has maintained your ongoing entrepreneurial focus?
3. What individual(s) have been models of inspiration for you throughout your entrepreneurial career and in what way? *[No need to mention a name, but please state if the person was a close friend, uncle, coworker, etc.]*
4. How has any formal education or training you have received (to whatever extent) been helpful? If so, in which way?
5. How many different business ventures have you started in the course of your entrepreneurial career?
6. What percentage of these business ventures do you estimate were financially successful?

II. Entrepreneurial Questions Regarding Your Primary Business

[If the entrepreneur has been involved in more than one business (which is likely), then have them focus on their most notable success or their current business (their "Primary Business").]

7. In order to provide some context, please describe your Primary Business: What does the company do? Who does

it sell to? What does it sell? What is your competitive advantage? What is the nature of your overall industry? *[Some or all of this information can be provided via the Company's web site or printed material.]*

8. How did you identify the opportunity that led to the setting up of your Primary Business?

9. What were the critical elements you assessed before you decided to pursue the opportunity? *[e.g., the competition? the market?]*

10. How much time did it take from seeing the opportunity to the first day of operation?

11. If you had partners, who were they, and how did you find them? *[e.g., family, friends professional advisors]*

12. Did you have a business plan of any kind (or any kind of written plan)?

13. What kind of financing did you have?

14. How much capital did it take?

15. How long did it take to reach a positive cash-flow position?

16. If you did not have enough money at the time of the start, or at low points in the business cycle, what were some things you did in order to stretch your capital?

17. What did you perceive to be the strengths (up to 3) of your venture?

18. What did you perceive to be the weaknesses (up to 3) of your venture?

19. What was your most satisfying accomplishment or event?

20. What was your most disappointing situation or event?

21. Once you got going, what were the most difficult gaps to fill and problems to solve as you began to grow your company?

22. What were the key attributes you looked for in people (partners, advisors, managers) as you grew the company?

III. Reflective Questions

23. What are some things that you have found to be most personally rewarding and satisfying for yourself as an entrepreneur?

24. What are ways in which you have developed your own entrepreneurial skills in order to be more effective as an entrepreneur *[e.g., time management; conflict resolution; financial analysis]?*

25. What are ways in which you cope with or manage the personal stress of being an entrepreneur *[e.g., reliance on spouse; friends]?*

26. What are the ways in which you have dealt with others who have disappointed you in business *[e.g., friend betraying you; employee cheating]?*

27. What do you think are the most important personal traits (up to 3) for an entrepreneur and why *[e.g., courage, integrity, prudence, passion, honestly, reliability]?*

28. What are the most important lessons you have learned with respect to starting and running a business that you pass on to an aspiring entrepreneur?
[This should not include faith-related issues, as this is dealt with in the following section; this should be 3–5 lessons.]

IV. Belief, Entrepreneurship & the Marketplace

29. How do you describe the impact of your calling in terms of how you find or define meaning in the context of your entrepreneurial pursuits *[e.g., do you use the term/ phrase "calling," identifying your "purpose," finding "God's will," or "God's leading"?]?*

30. Who, if any one, affirmed your sense of direction in your entrepreneurial pursuits (as described in Question #29 above) *[e.g., pastor, mentor, the church, friends]?*

31. As a result of being an entrepreneur, how has your approach to entrepreneurship changed *[e.g., I am more forgiving, more gracious, more generous, more determined]*?

32. How did you (or do you) integrate your business/ entrepreneurship expertise with your commitment (and how are they complementary)?

33. How have you been involved in your local church (that you now attend and the ones you have attended in the past)? Are these involvements related to your business expertise?

34. Have you been involved in your denomination, and how?

35. Have you been involved in parachurch organizations, and how?

36. What are some examples *[e.g., situations with partners, suppliers, customers]* of how you have integrated principles into your business practices and thus acted differently due to your faith?

37. What are the most important lessons (up to 3) you have learned that you believe are important for those pursuing entrepreneurship?

38. How could the church/religious institutions in a general sense (e.g., a local congregation) support you in applying your faith in the context of entrepreneurship?

39. What have been the most significant challenges for you pursuing entrepreneurship?

40. Who was most helpful (and why or how) in addressing these challenges: church leadership, friends, etc.?

41. Have you hired people from your inner circle? If so, has that been a positive or negative experience?

42. Have you done business with other people in your inner circle, and how *[e.g., mentoring, in partnership, buying products, giving them referrals]*?

43. Has your relationship with those people you have done business with been positively or negatively

affected—from a business and spiritual standpoint—by doing business together, and how?

44. What do you believe are appropriate means to share your faith in your company?

45. Is there any particular passage(s) of scripture or wisdom that you have found particularly meaningful or that is inspirational to you?

46. Do you have any questions or comments related to entrepreneurs that you would like to express an opinion on and that were not covered in this questionnaire?

THANK YOU VERY MUCH FOR YOUR PARTICIPATION!

Works Cited

Allen, Marc. 1995. *Visionary Business: Entrepreneur's Guide to Success.* Novato, CA: New World Library.

Amabile, Teresa, and Steven J. Kramer. 2012. "How Leaders Kill Meaning at Work." *McKinsey Quarterly*, no. 1: 124–131.

Amortegui, Jessica. 2014. "Why Finding Meaning at Work is More Important Than Feeling Happy." *Fast Company.* https://www.fastcompany.com/3032126/how-to-find-meaning-during-your-pursuit-of-happiness-at-work

Bokhari, Allum. 2016. "Former Facebook Employee Compares Company Culture To A Religion."

Breitbart. http://www.breitbart.com/tech/2016/06/06/former-facebook-employee-compares-company-culture-to-a-religion/

Canfield, Jack, Mark Victor Hansen, and Les Hewitt. 2000. *The Power of Focus.* Deerfield Beach, FL: Health Communications.

Colson, C.W., and N. Pearcey. 1999. *How Now Shall We Live?* Carol Stream, IL: Tyndale House Publishers.

Constantineau, Bruce. "Companies Like Lululemon Take Different Approach to Relationships with Employees." *Vancouver Sun.* www.vancouversun.com. Accessed August 16, 2017.

Dik, Bryan J., and Ryan D. Duffy. 2012. *Make Your Job A Calling: How The Psychology of Vocation Can Change Your Life At Work.* West Conshohocken, PA: Templeton.

Ferguson, Niall. 2011. *Civilization: The West and the Rest.* New York, NY: Penguins Books.

Frankl, Viktor E. 2006. *Man's Search for Meaning.* Boston, MA: Beacon Press. Originally published in 1959.

Goossen, Richard J., ed. 2008. *Entrepreneurial Leaders: Reflections on Faith At Work.* Langley, BC: Trinity Western University.

Green, Stephen. 2010. *Good Value: Reflections on Money, Morality and an Uncertain World*. New York, NY: Grove Atlantic.

Grenz, Stanley. 1996. *A Primer on Postmodernism*. Grand Rapids, MI: Eerdmans.

Handy, Charles. 1997. "The Search for Meaning: A Conversation with Charles Handy." *Leader to Leader Institute*, No. 5.

Izzo, John B., and Eric Klein. 1997. *Awakening Corporate Soul: Four Paths To Unleash The Power of People At Work*. Vancouver, Canada: Fairwinds Press.

Kantor, Jodi, and David Streitfield. 2015. "Inside Amazon: Wrestling Big Ideas in Bruising Workplace."

New York Times. https://www.nytimes.com/2015/08/16/technology/inside -amazon-wrestling-big-ideas-in-a-bruising-workplace.html?mcubz=0

Knight, Phil. 2016. *Shoe Dog: A Memoir by The Creator of NIKE*. New York, NY: Simon & Schuster.

Lockwood, Rene. 2011. "Religiosity Rejected: Exploring the Religo-Social Dimensions of Landmark Education." *International Journal for the Study of New Religions*. 2.2: 225 -254.

Maxwell, John C. 2007. *Be All You Can Be: A Challenge to Stretch Your God-given Potential*. Colorado Springs, CO: David C. Cook.

_____. 2015. *Intentional Living: Choosing a Life That Matters*. New York, NY: Center Street, an imprint of Hachette Book Group.

May, Douglas R., Richard L. Gilson, and Lynn M. Harter. 2004. "The psychological conditions of meaningfulness, safety and availability and the engagement of the human spirit at work. *Journal of Occupational and Organizational Psychology*.

McGrath, Alistair. 2015. *Mere Apologetics*. Ada, Michigan: Baker Books.

Micklethwait, John, and Adrian Wooldridge. 2009. *God Is Back: How the Global Revival of Faith Is Changing the World*. New York, NY: Penguin Books.

Mitroff, Ian, and Elizabeth Denton. 2008. *A Spiritual Audit of Corporate America*. Jossey-Bass, an imprint of Wiley.

Newport, J.P. 1998. *The New Age Movement and the Biblical Worldview*. Grand Rapids, MI: Eerdmans.

Pink, Daniel H. 2009. *Drive: The Surprising Truth About What Motives Us*. New York, NY: Riverhead Books.

Pollard, C. William. 2014. *The Tides of Life: Learning to Lead and Serve as You Navigate the Currents of Life*. Wheaton, IL: Crossway.

Ramachandra, Vinoth. 1996. *Gods That Fail: Modern Idolatry and Christian Mission.* Downers Grove, IL: InterVarsity Press.

Stark, Rodney. 2015. *The Triumph of Faith: Why The World is More Religious Than Ever.* Wilmington, DE: Intercollegiate Studies Institute.

The "New Age" Religion: In General. www.procinwarn.com/newage general.htm. Accessed August 13, 2017.

Timmons, Jeffry A., and Stephen Spinelli. 2009. *New Venture Creation: Entrepreneurship for the 21st Century.* New York, NY: McGraw Hill/ Irwin.

Weber, Max. 2003. *The Protestant Ethic and the Spirit of Capitalism.* Foreword by R.H. Tawney. Mineola, NY: Dover. (First published by Max Weber in 1904–05.)

Wildeboer, Rob. "A Christian Perspective on Work." ELO Blog, December 7, 2015. http://www.entrepreneurialleaders.com/blog/67/ Being-An-Ambassador-for-Christ-At-Work.

Index